W9-ANC-237

Frogcatchers

Jeff Lemire

Gallery 13

New York   London   Toronto   Sydney   New Delhi

Gallery 13
An Imprint of Simon & Schuster, Inc.
1230 Avenue of the Americas
New York, NY 10020

First Gallery 13 hardcover edition January 2019

GALLERY 13 and colophon are trademarks of Simon & Schuster, Inc.

For information about special discounts for bulk purchases, please contact Simon & Schuster Special Sales at 1-866-506-1949 or business@simonandschuster.com.

The Simon & Schuster Speakers Bureau can bring authors to your live event. For more information or to book an event, contact the Simon & Schuster Speakers Bureau at 1-866-248-3049 or visit our website at www.simonspeakers.com.

Manufactured in the United States of America

1   3   5   7   9   10   8   6   4   2

Library of Congress Cataloging-in-Publication Data is available.

ISBN 978-1-9821-0737-6
ISBN 978-1-9821-0739-0 (ebook)

Frogcatchers

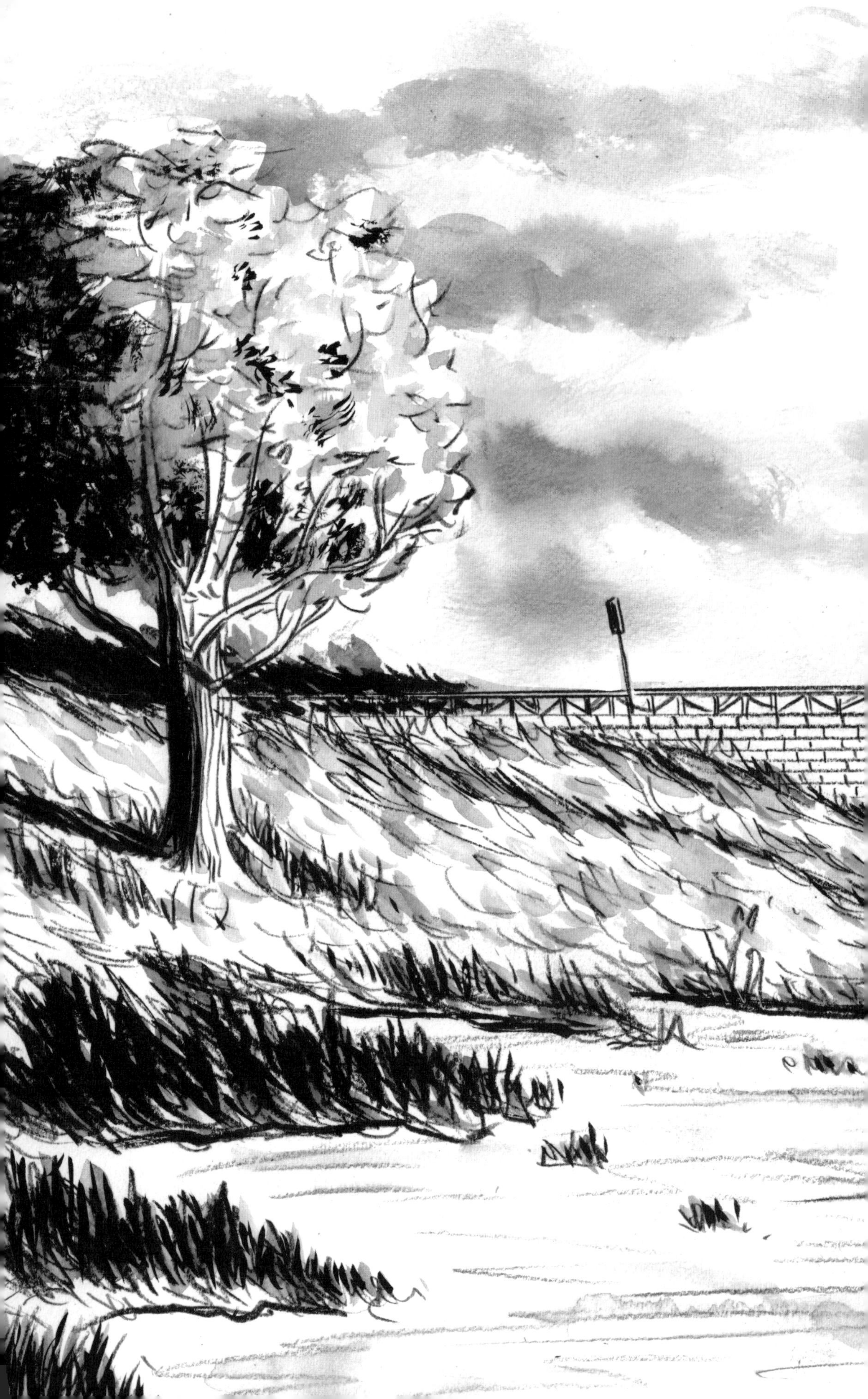

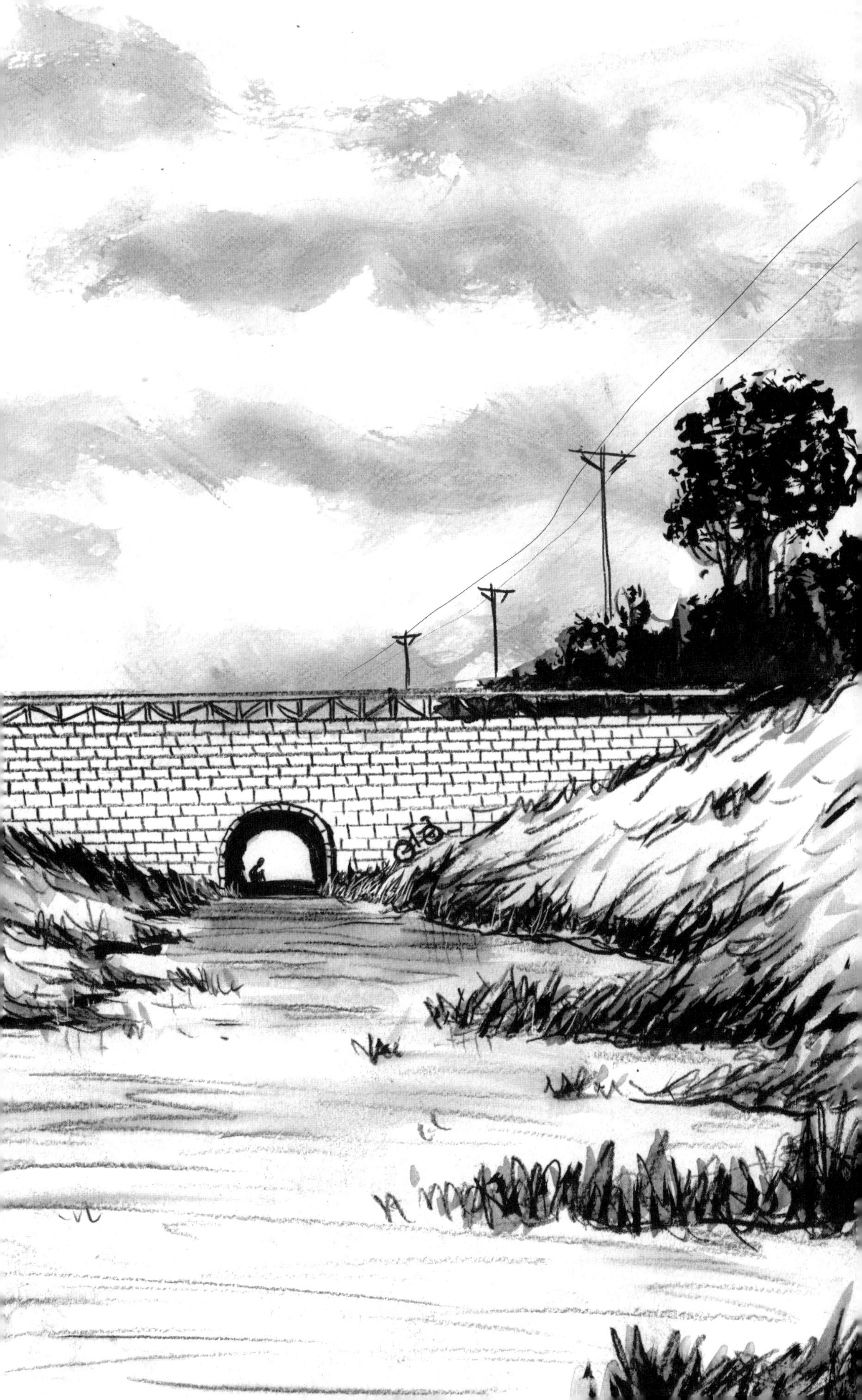

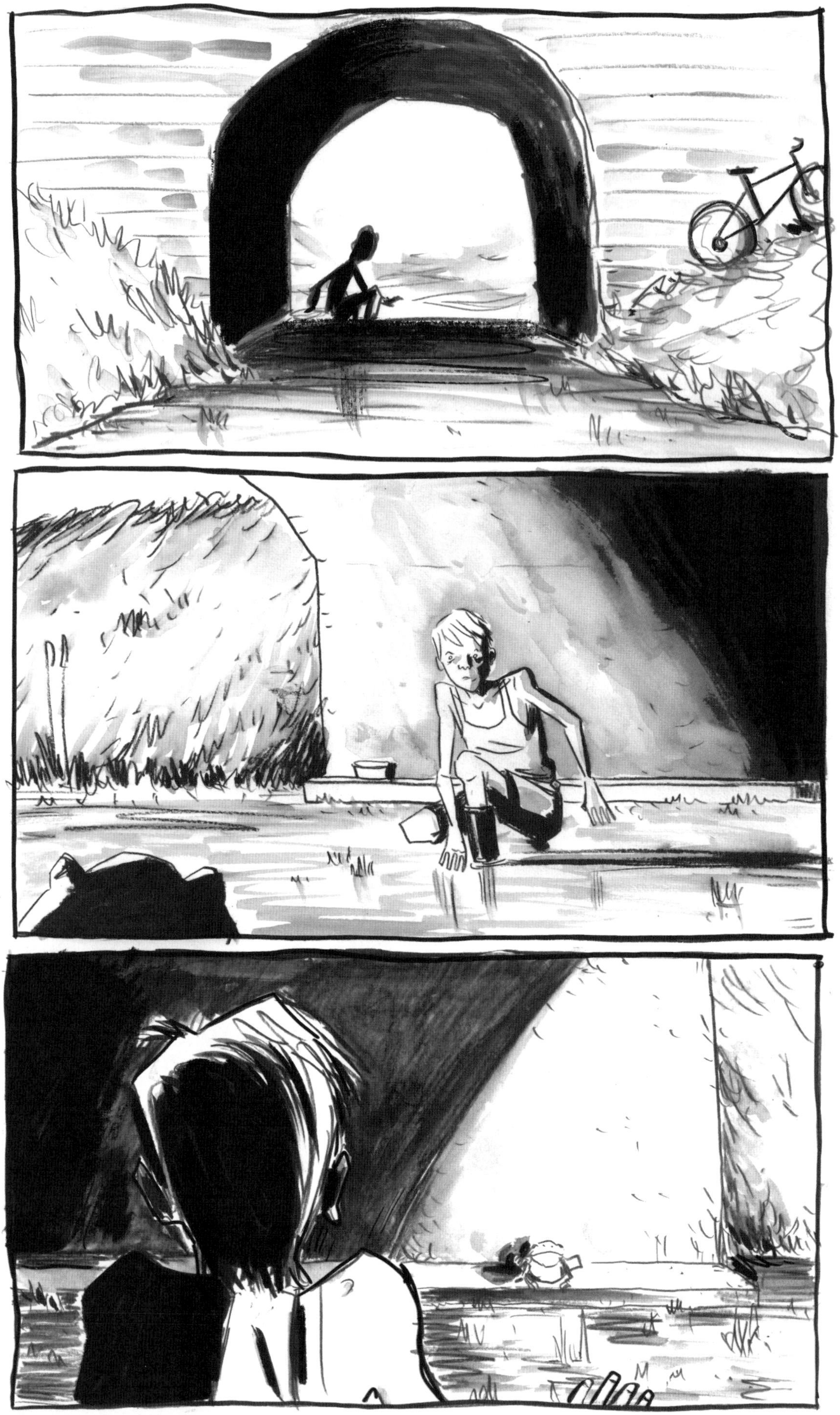

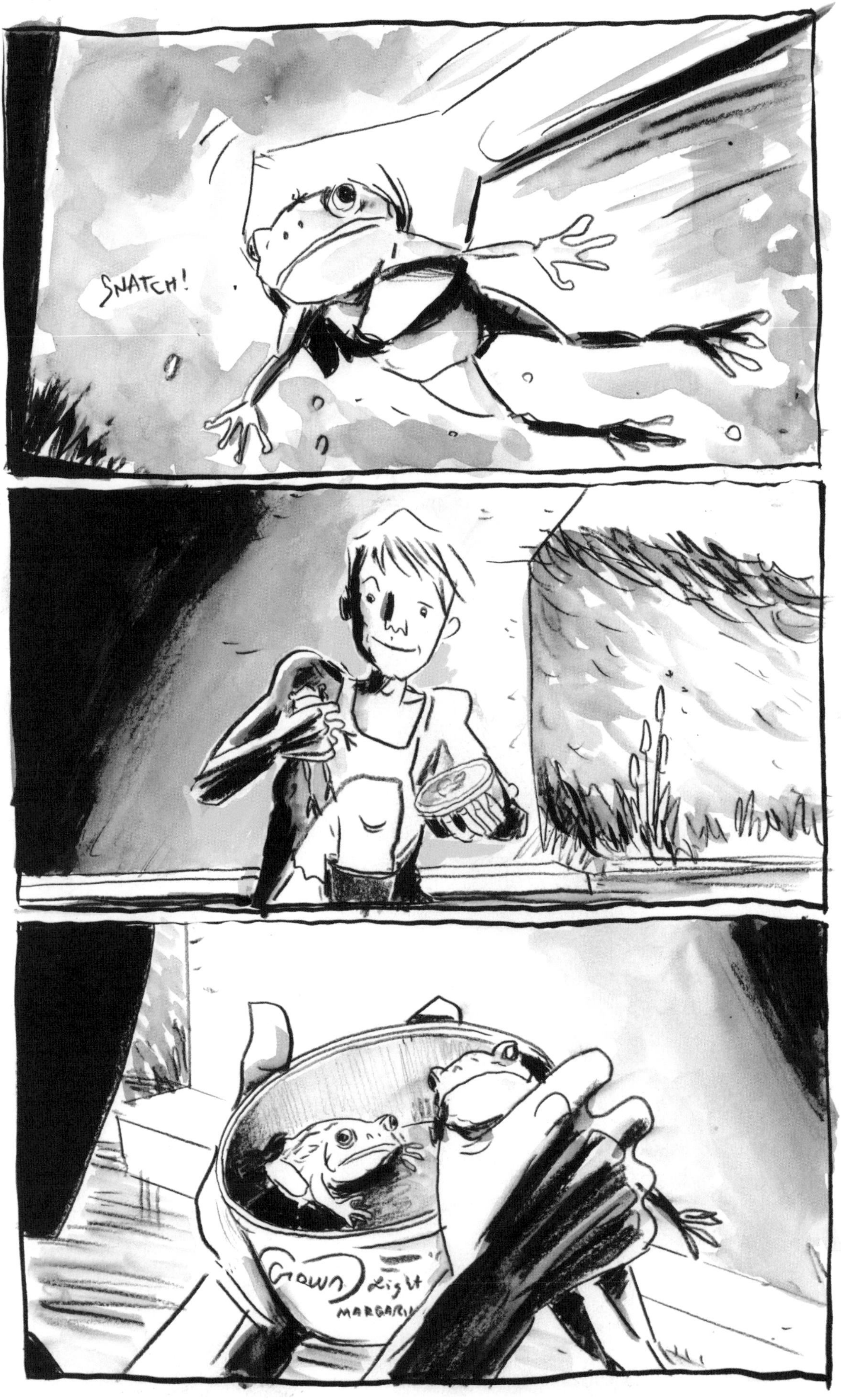
SNATCH!
Crown Light

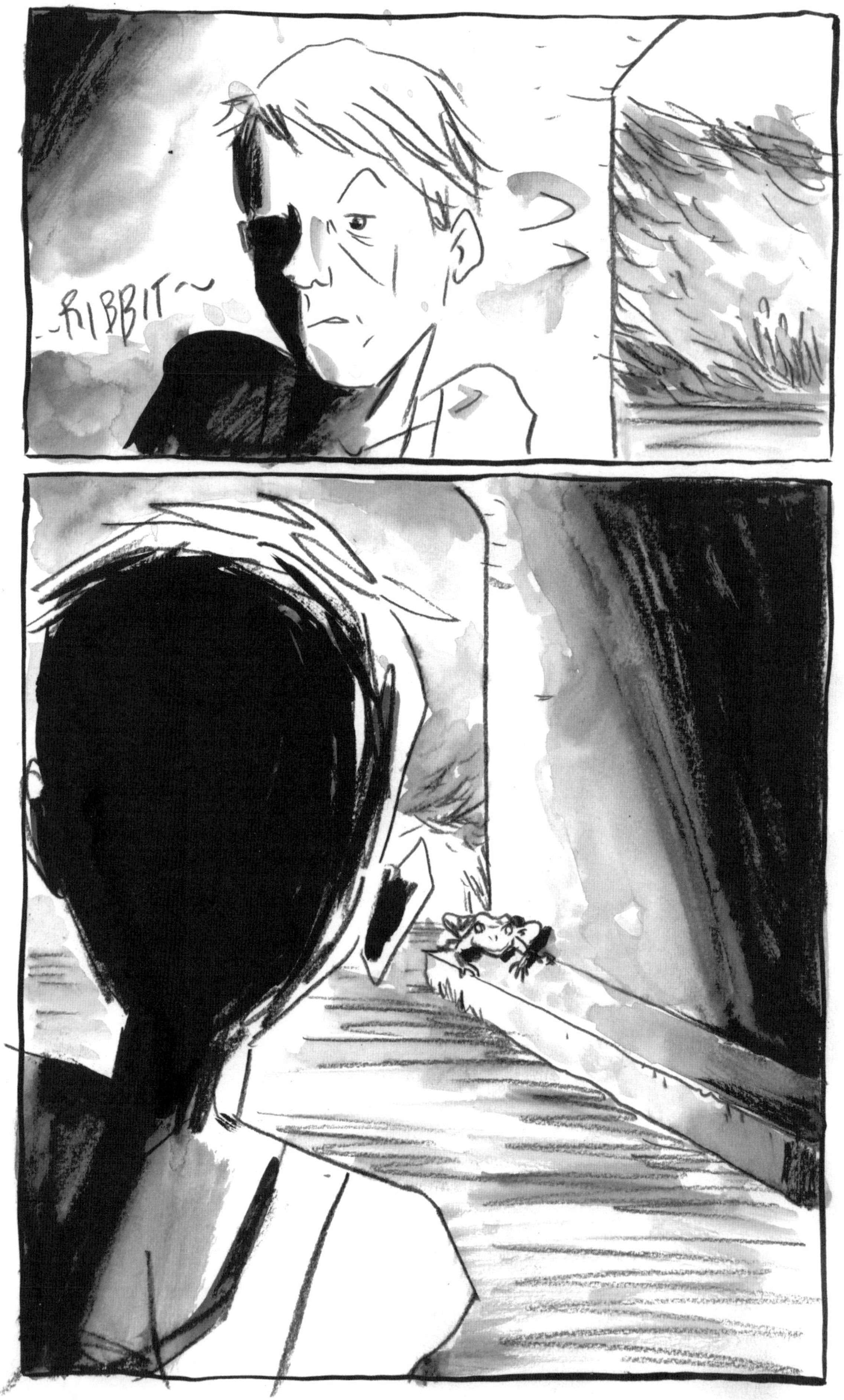
--RIBBIT~

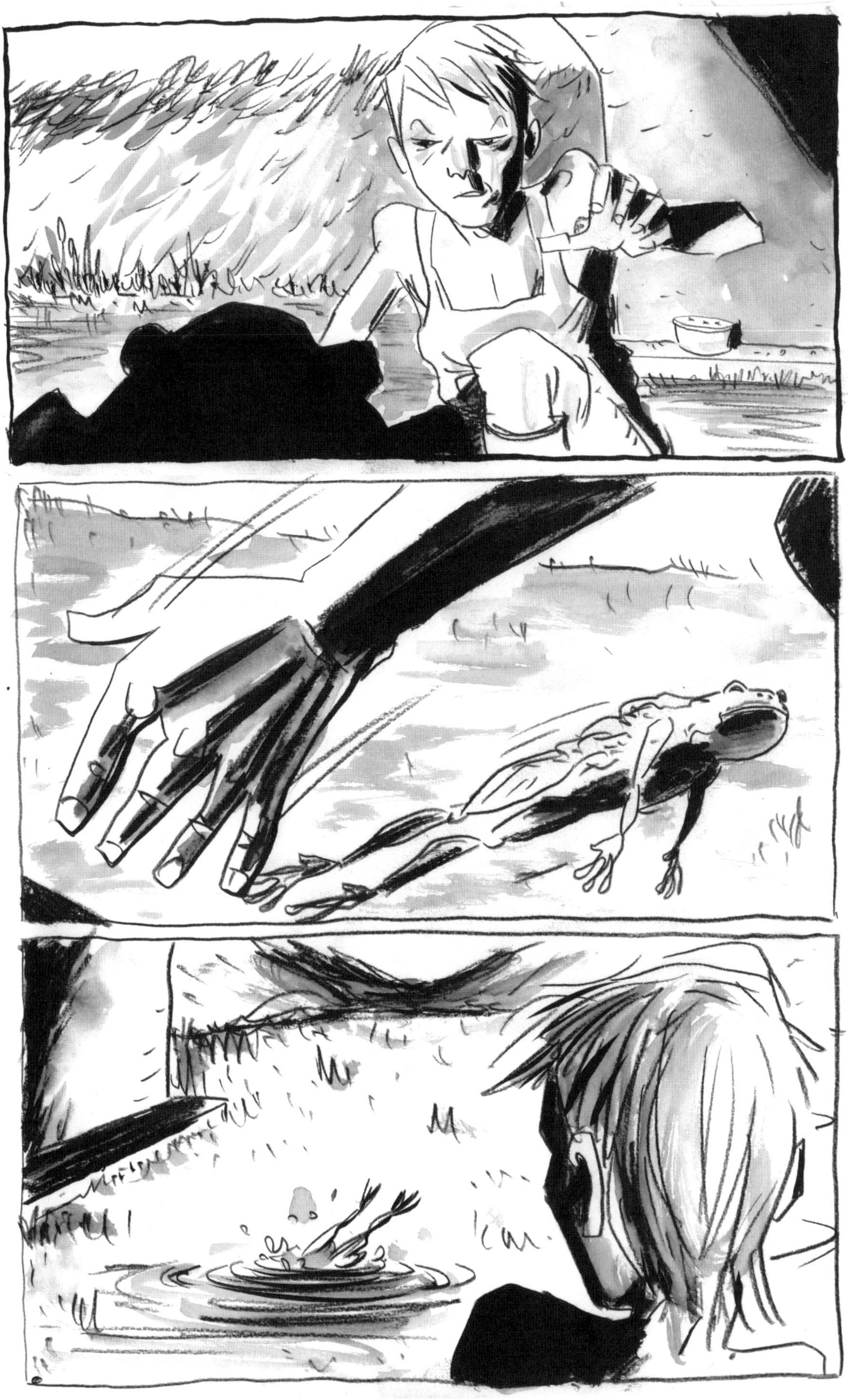

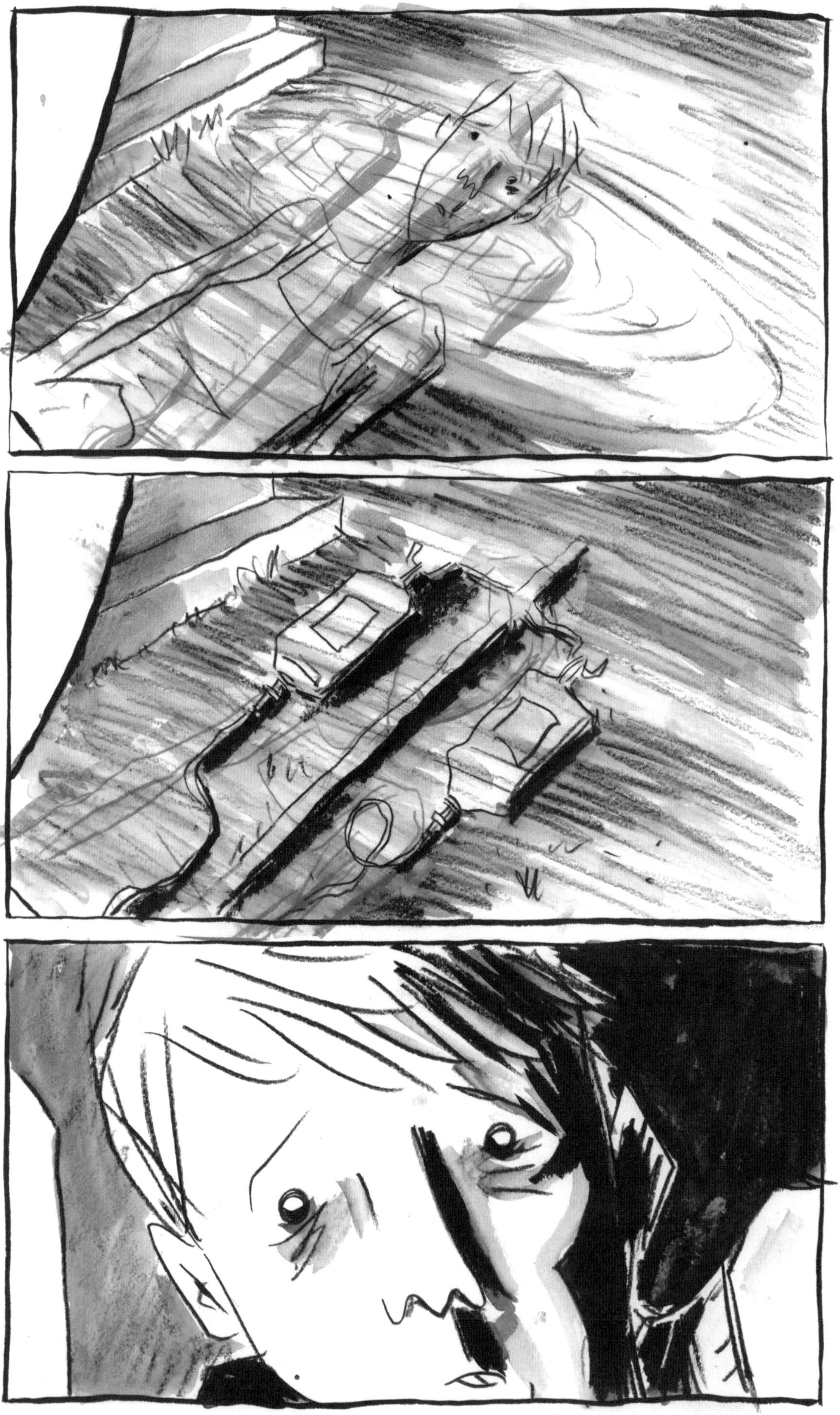

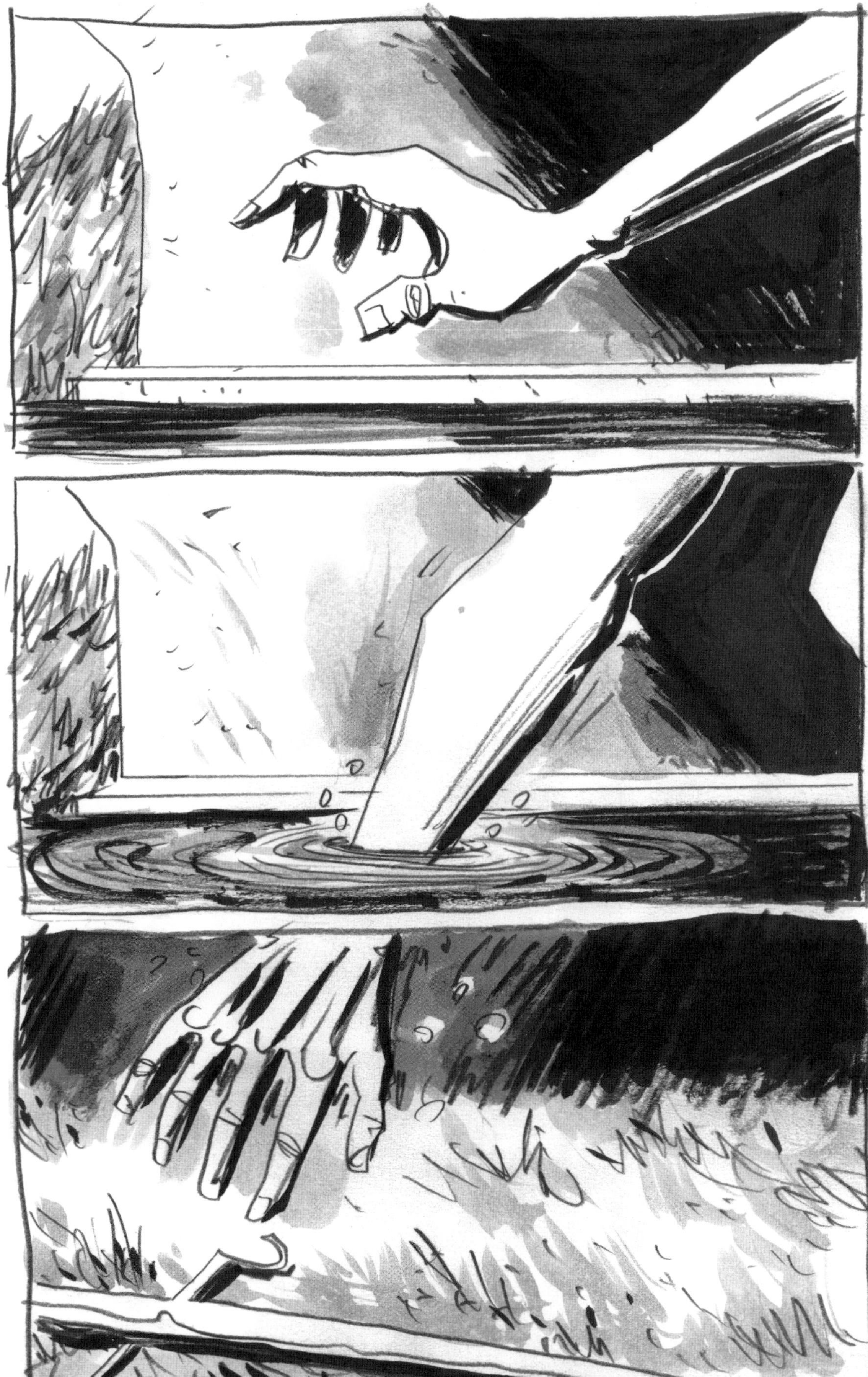

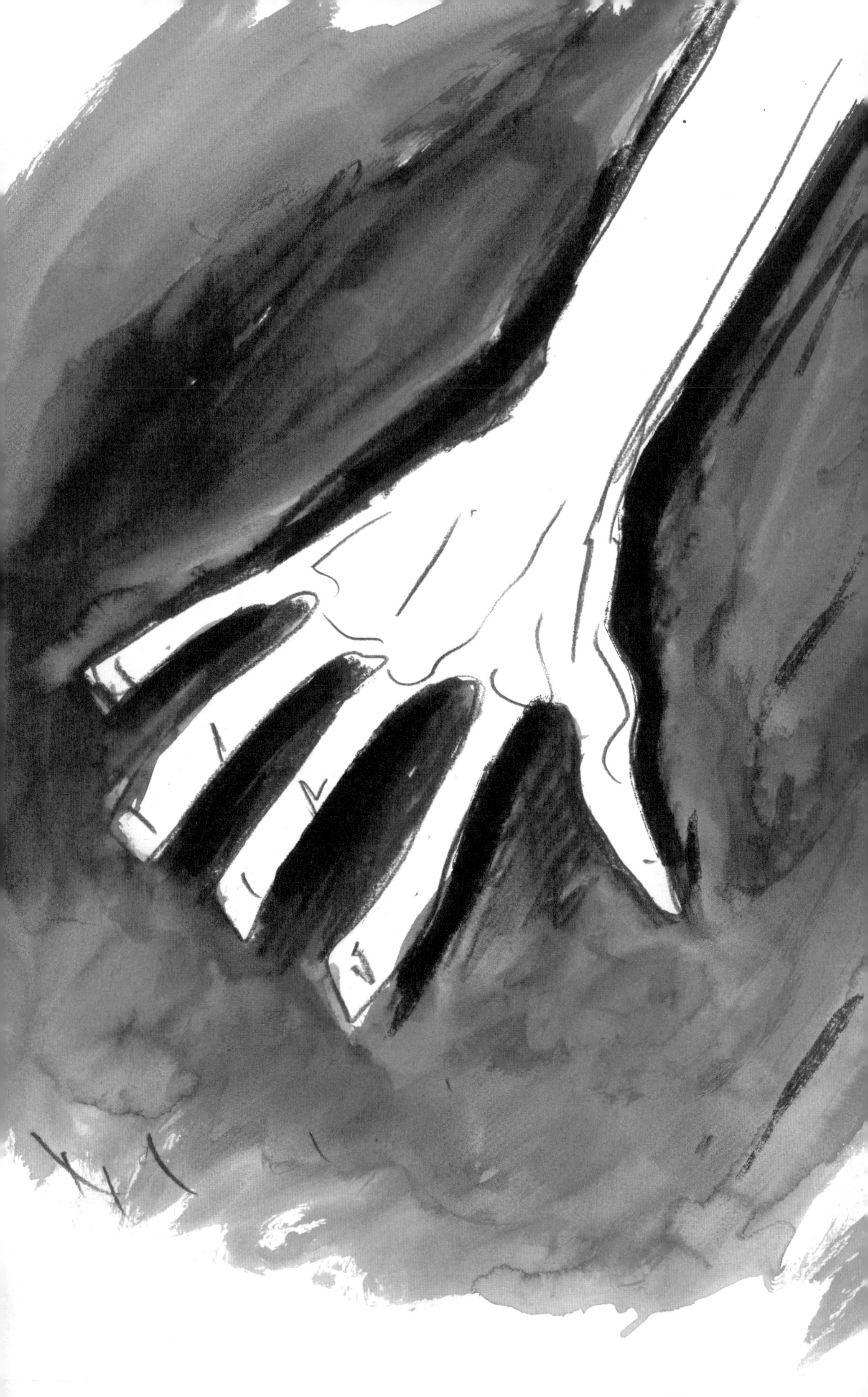

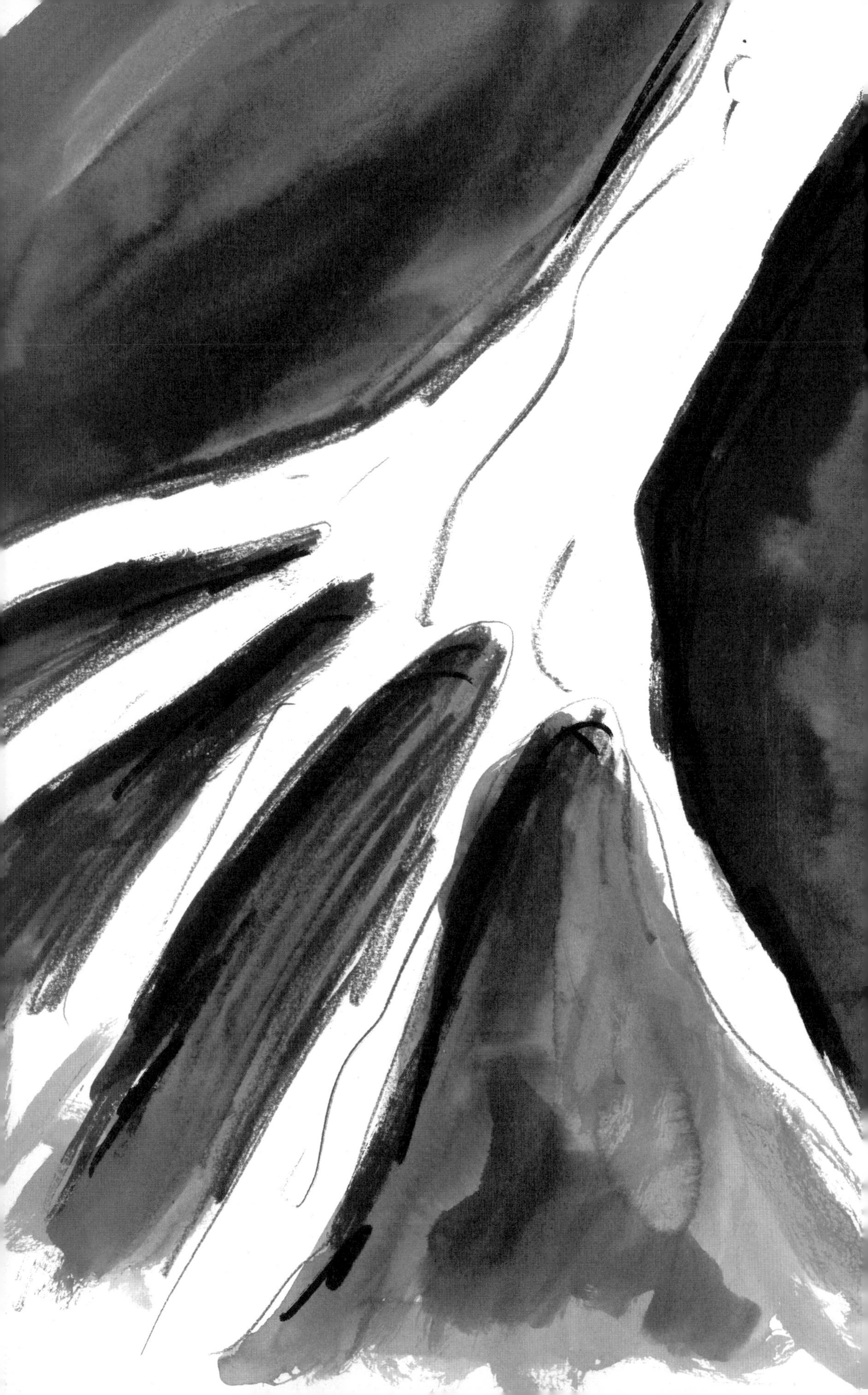

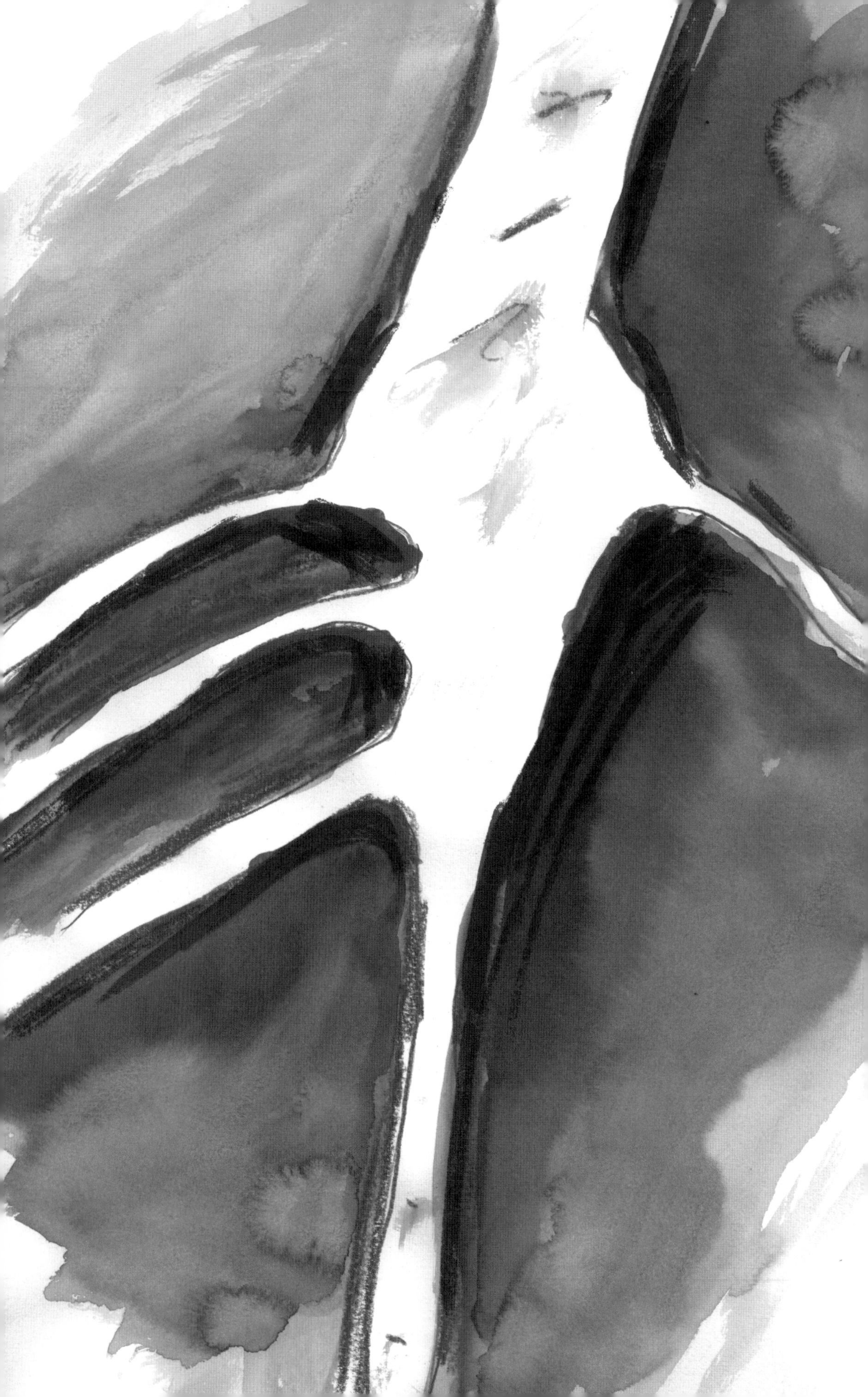

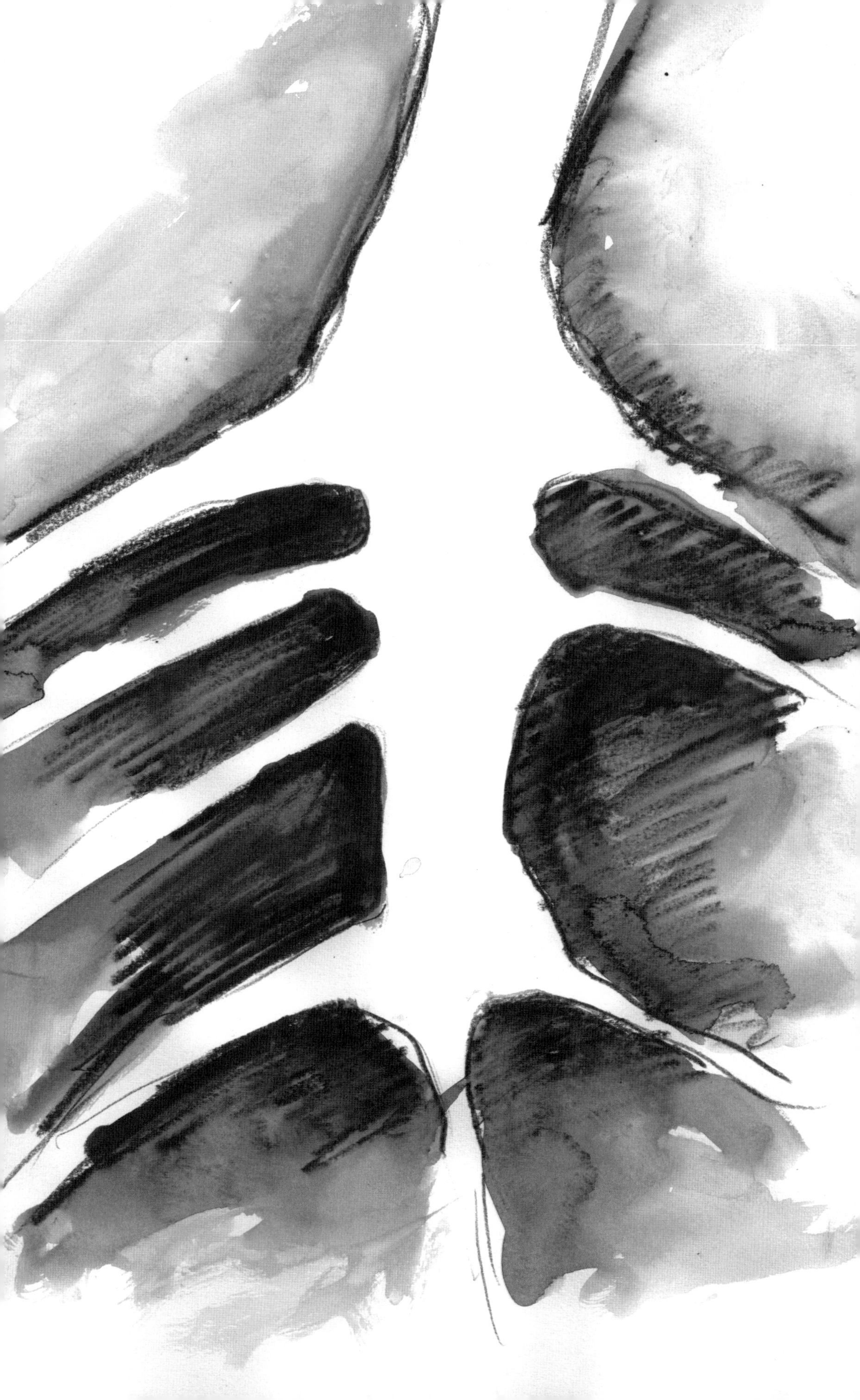

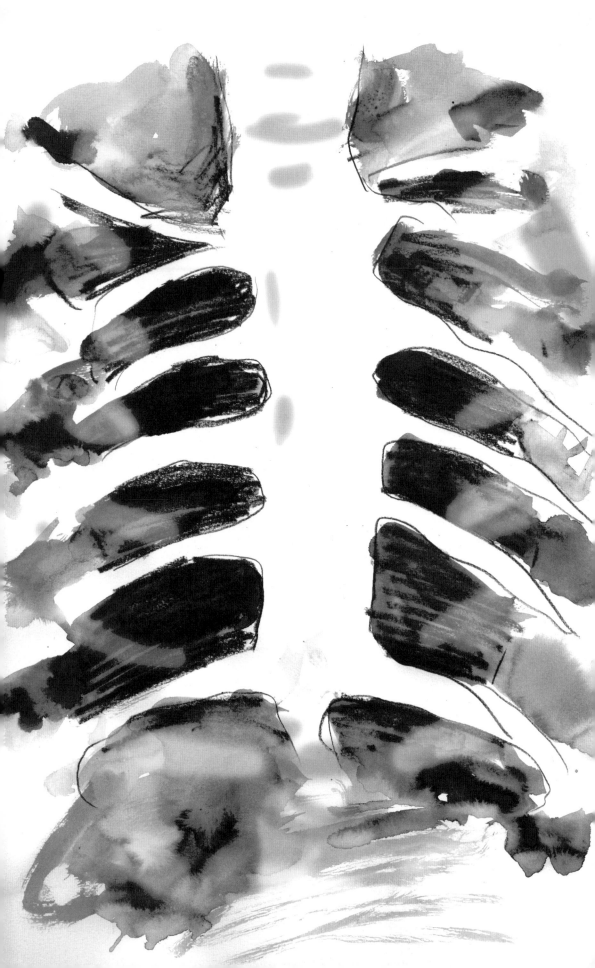

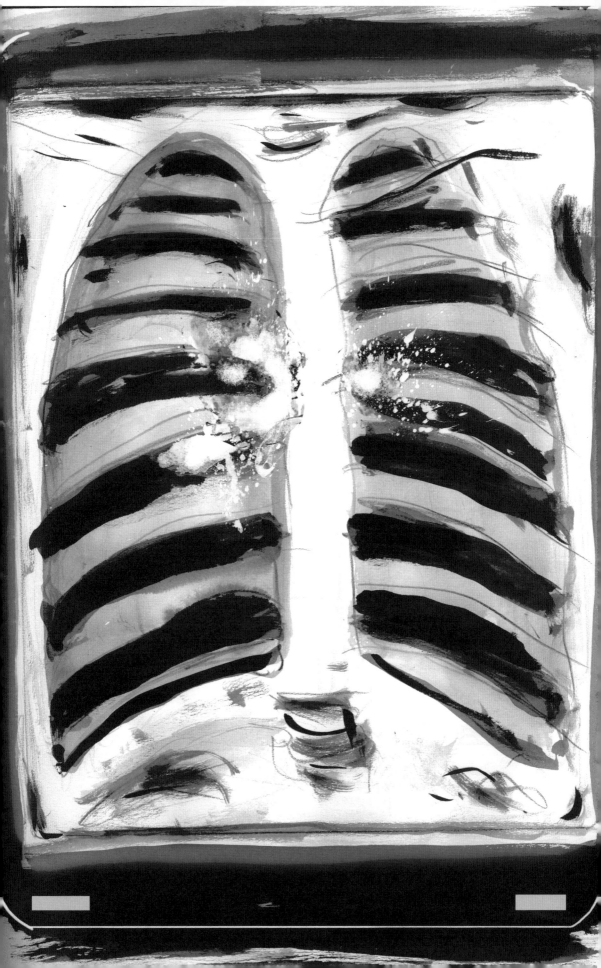

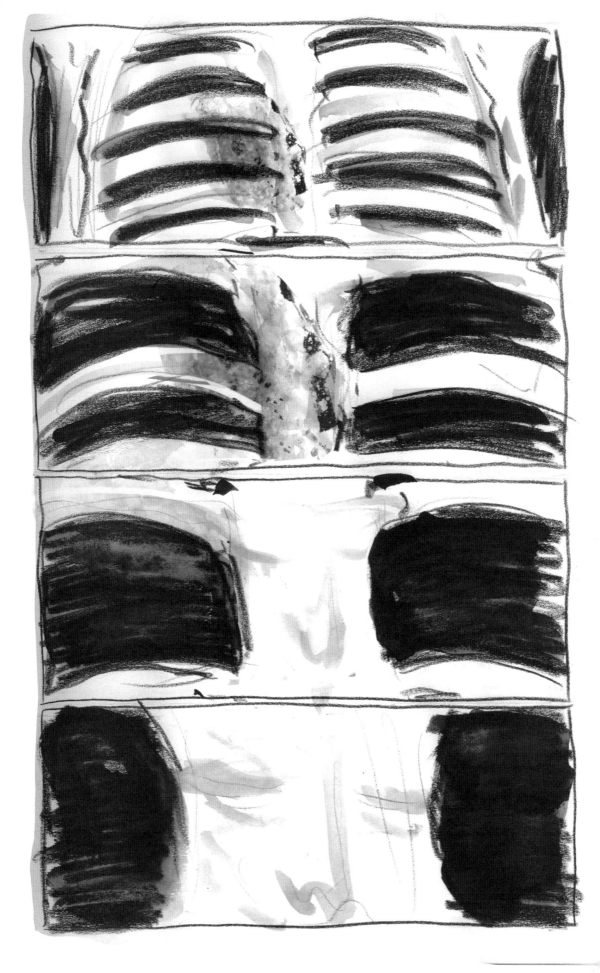

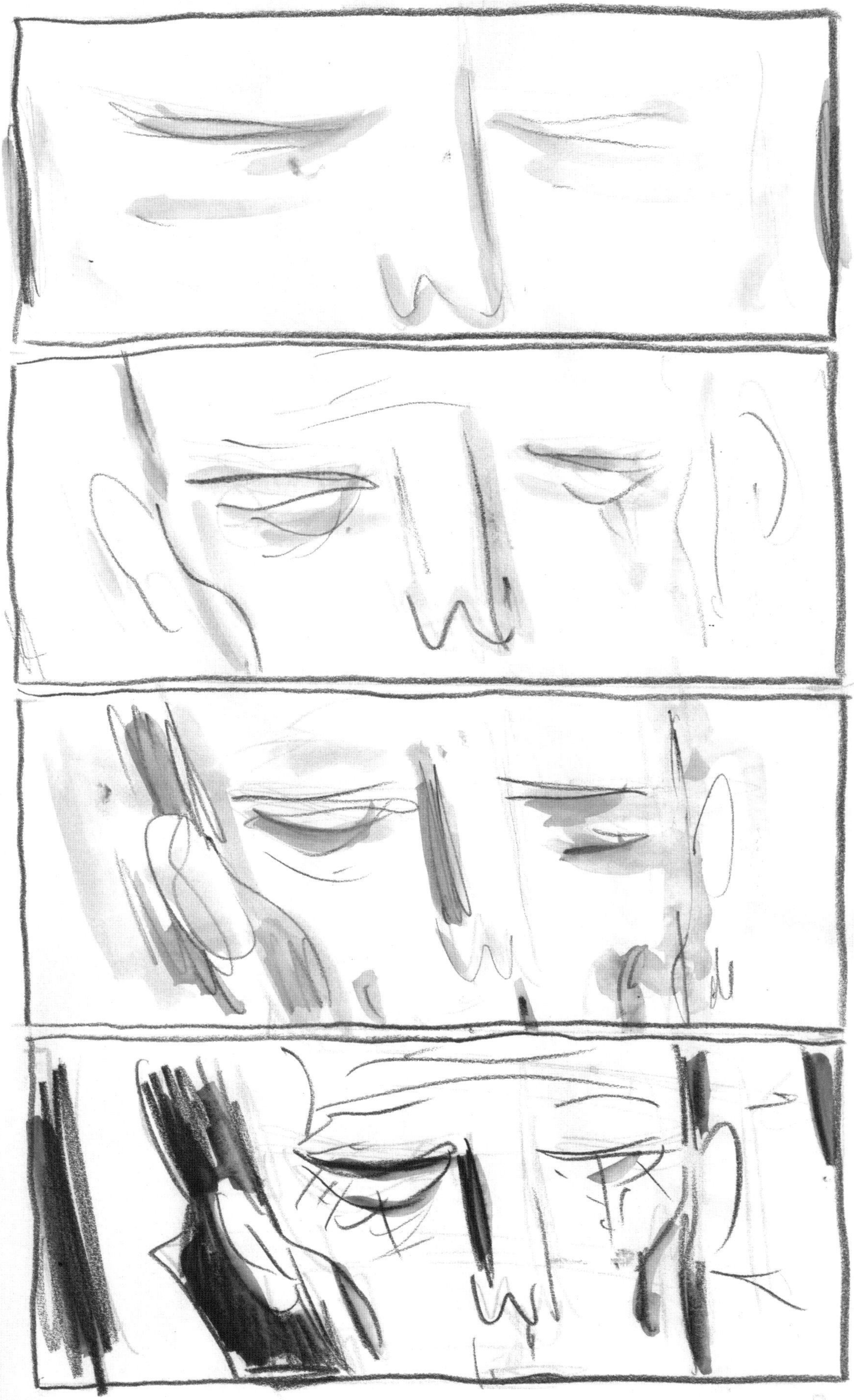

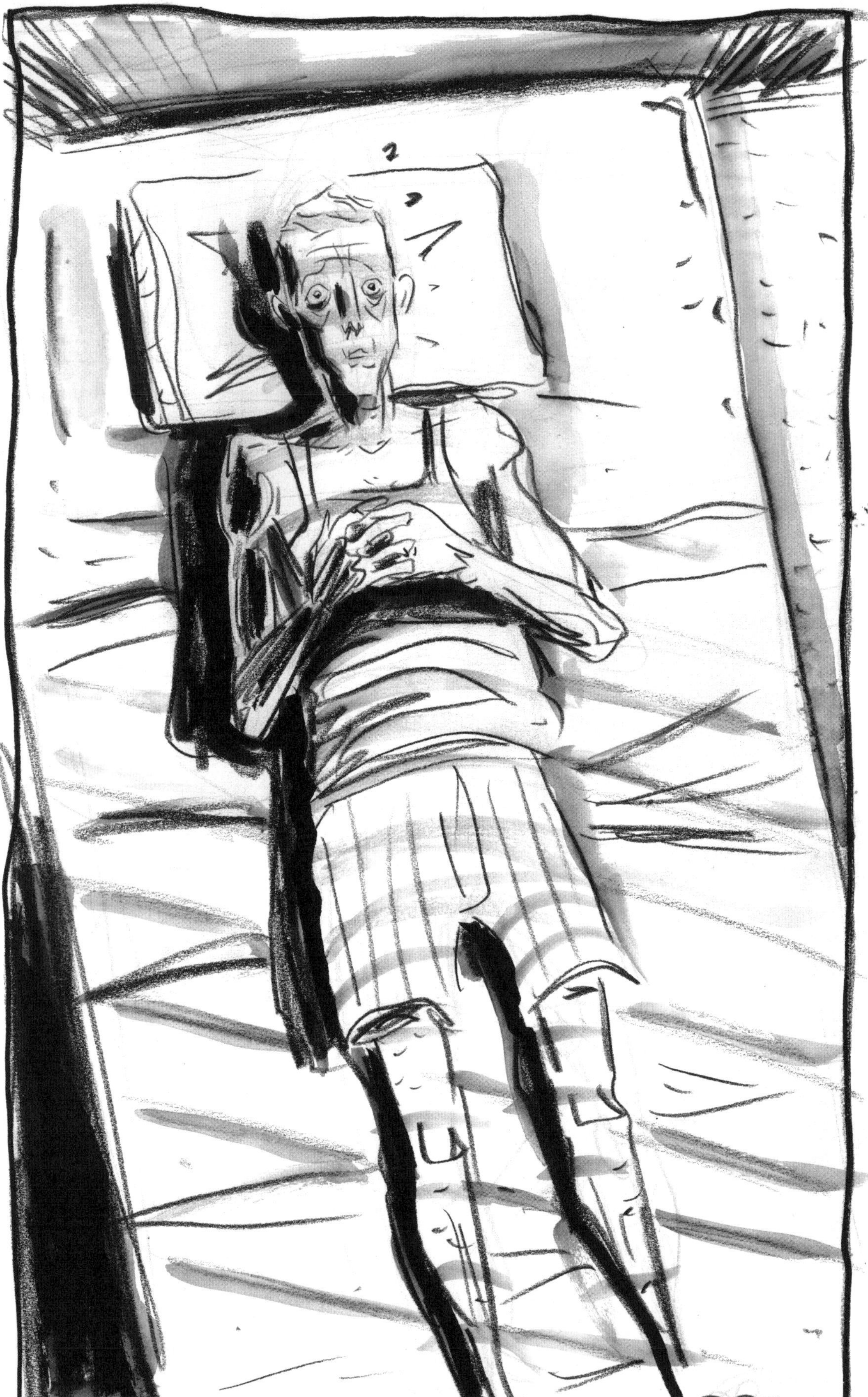

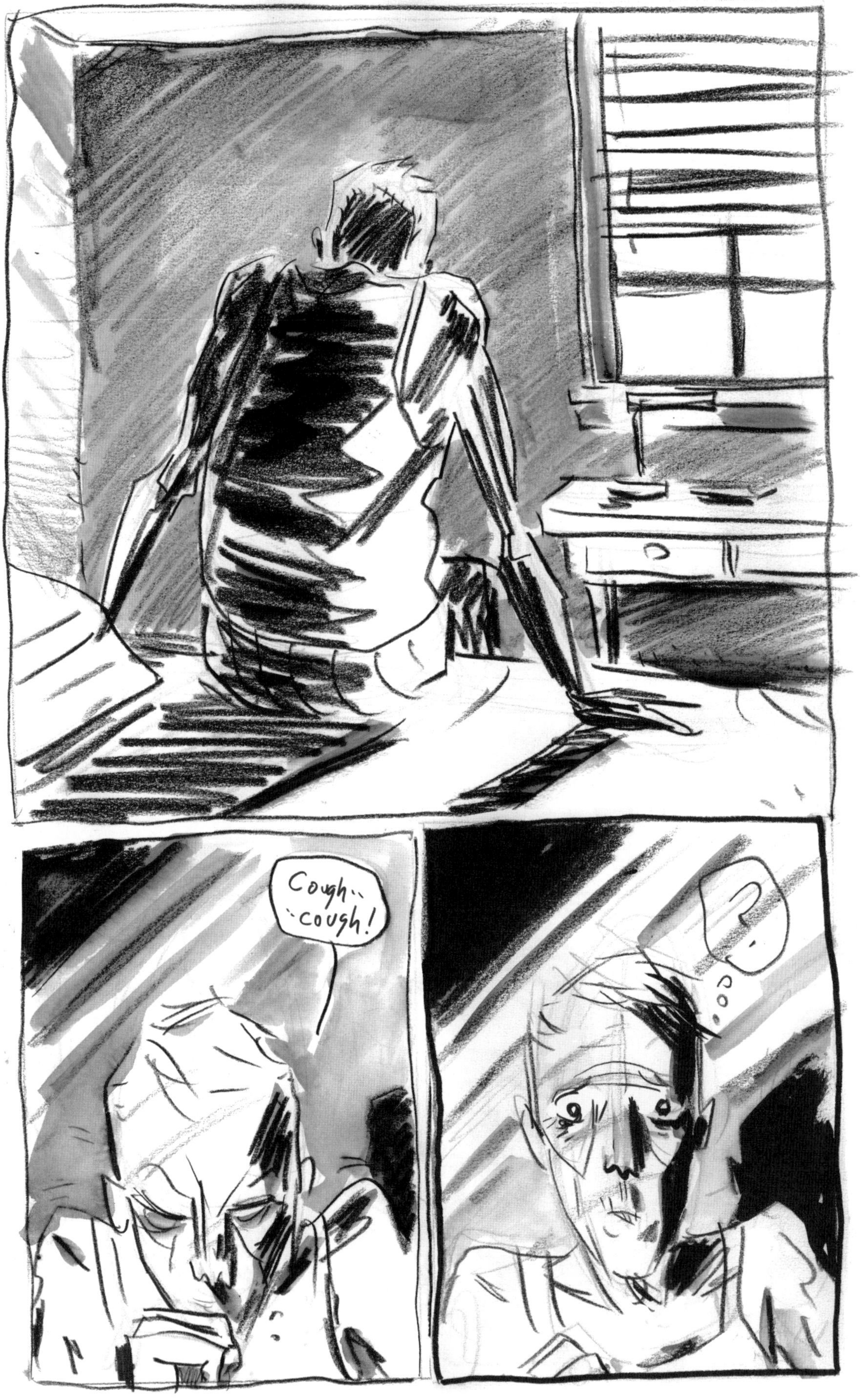
Cough..
..cough!
?

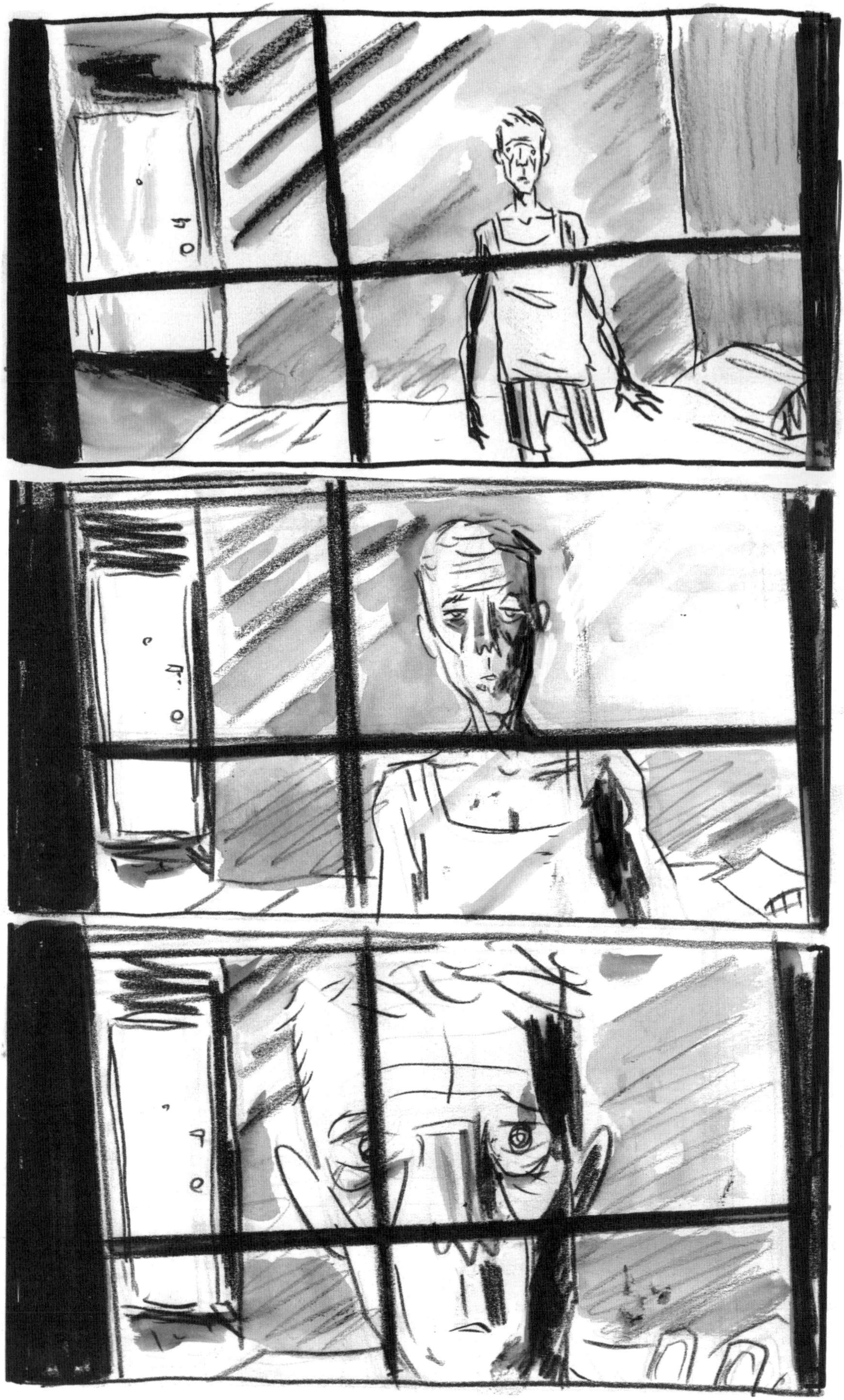

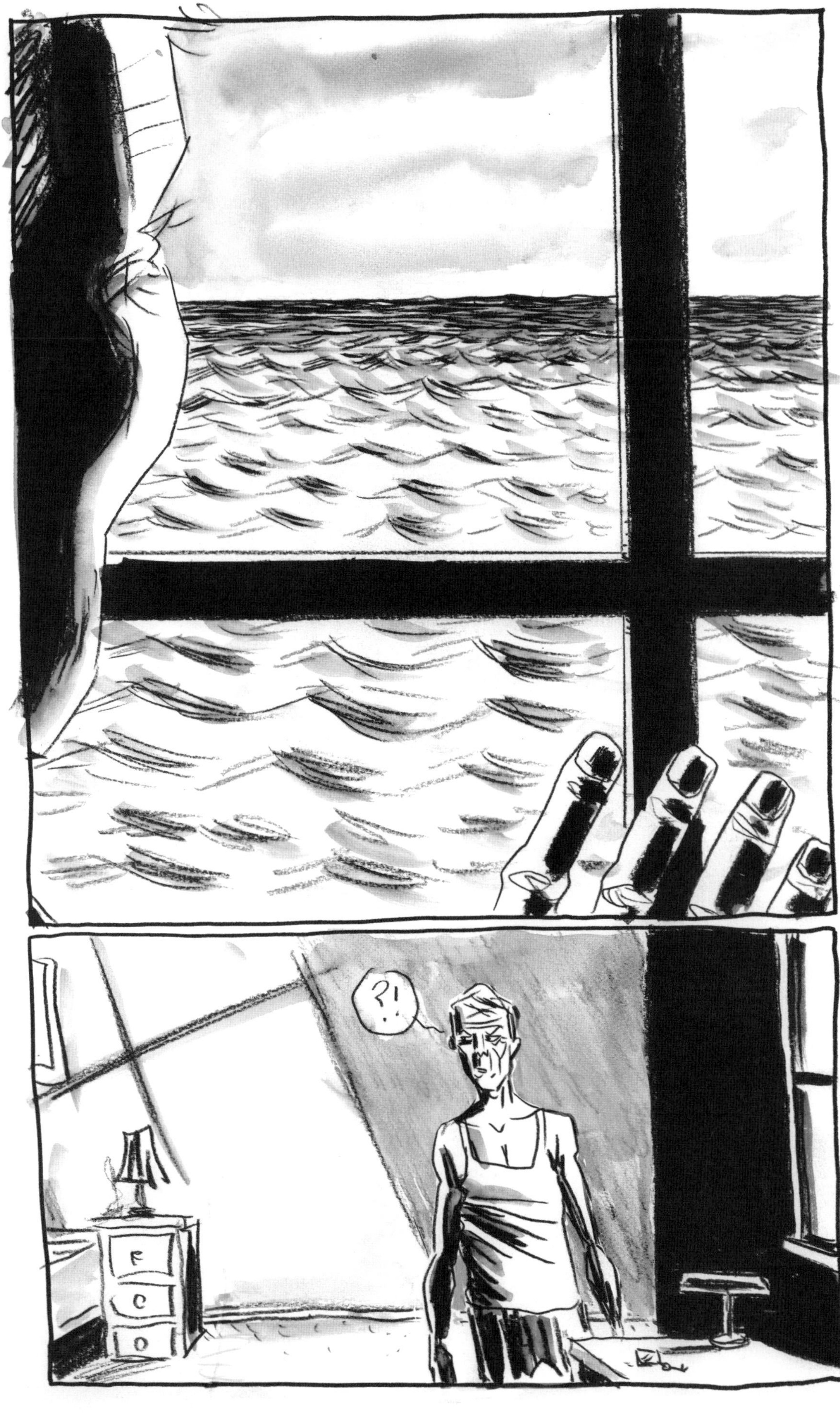
?!

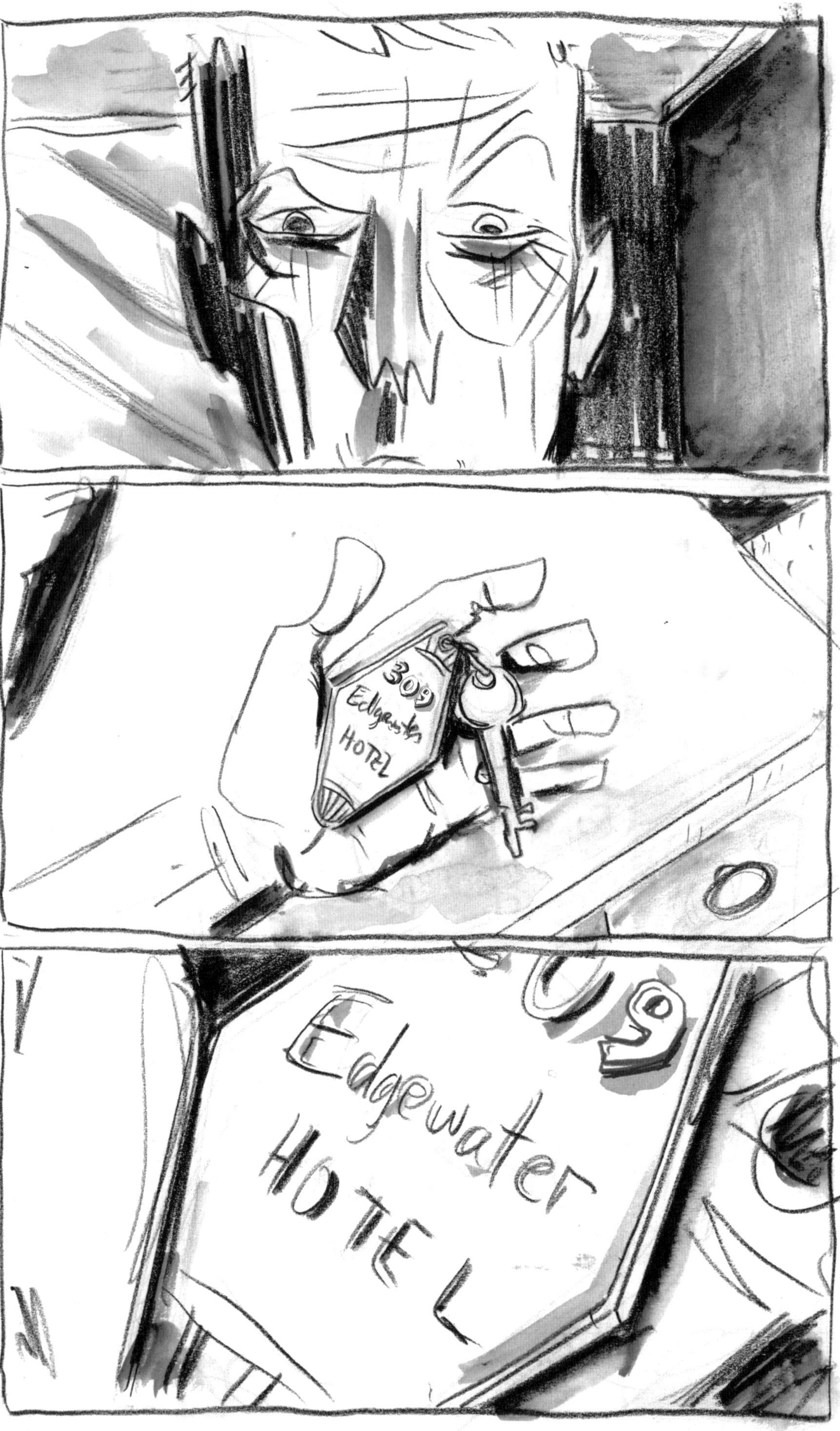
309
Edgewater
HOTEL
Edgewater
HOTEL

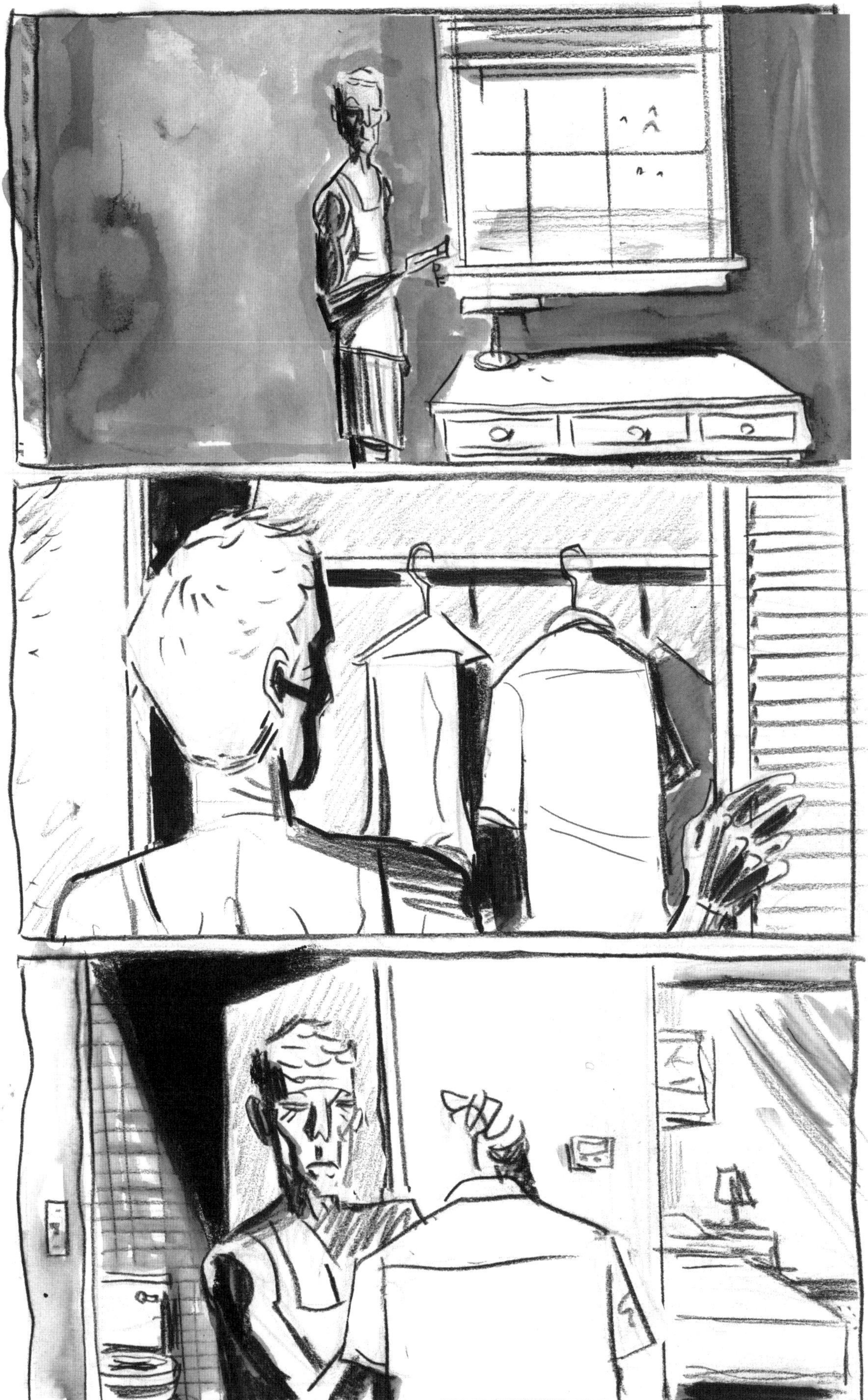

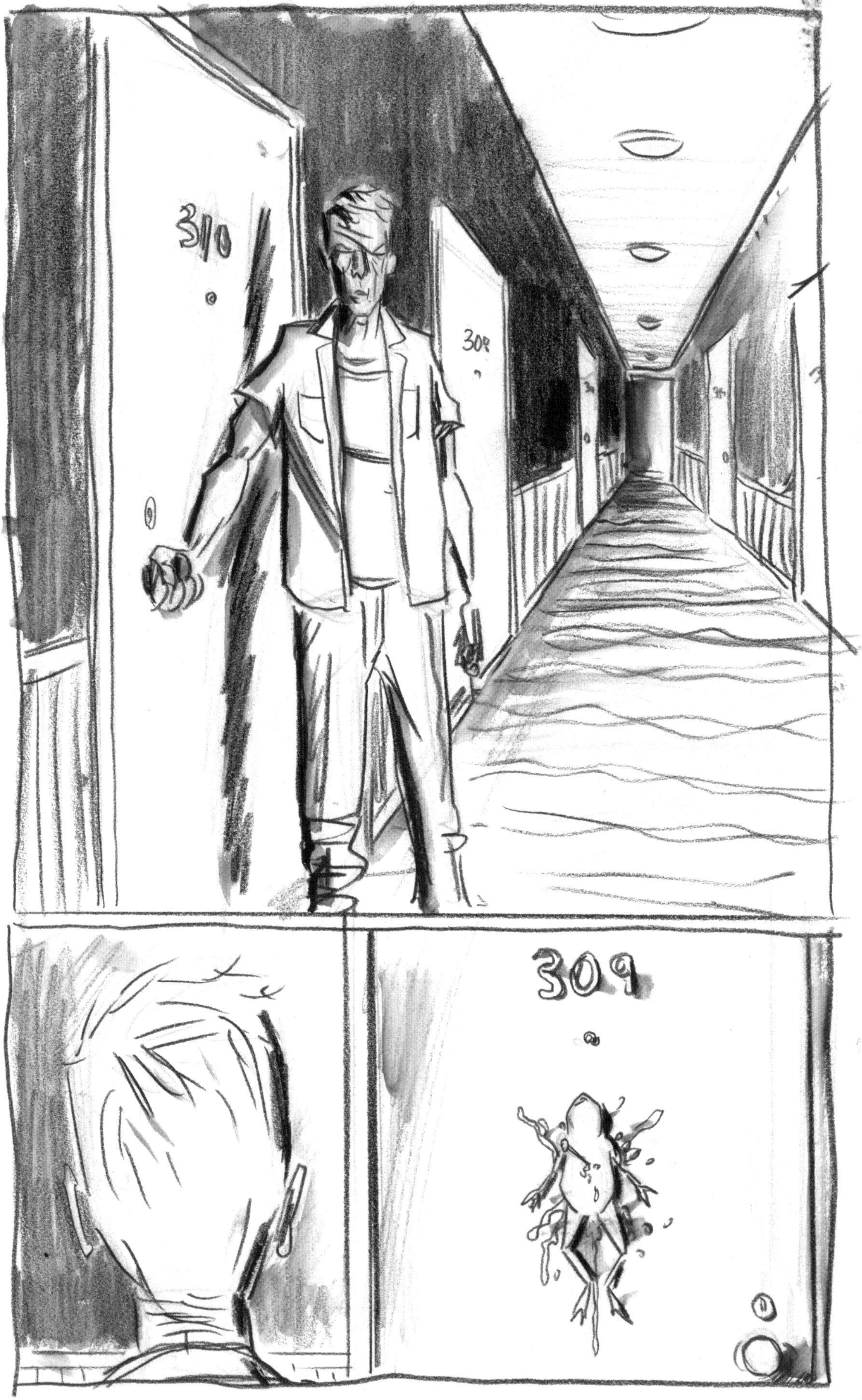
310
309
309

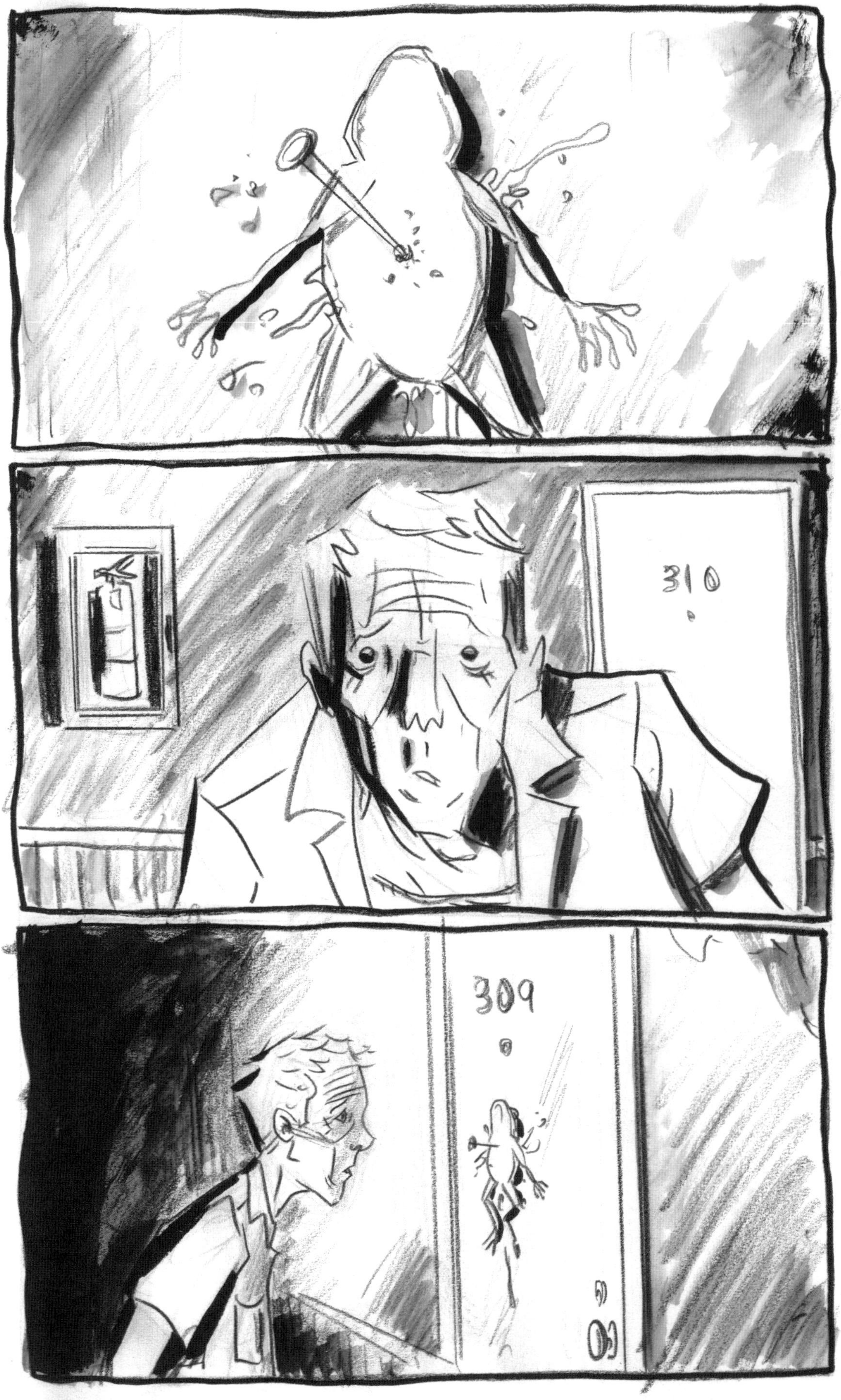
310
309

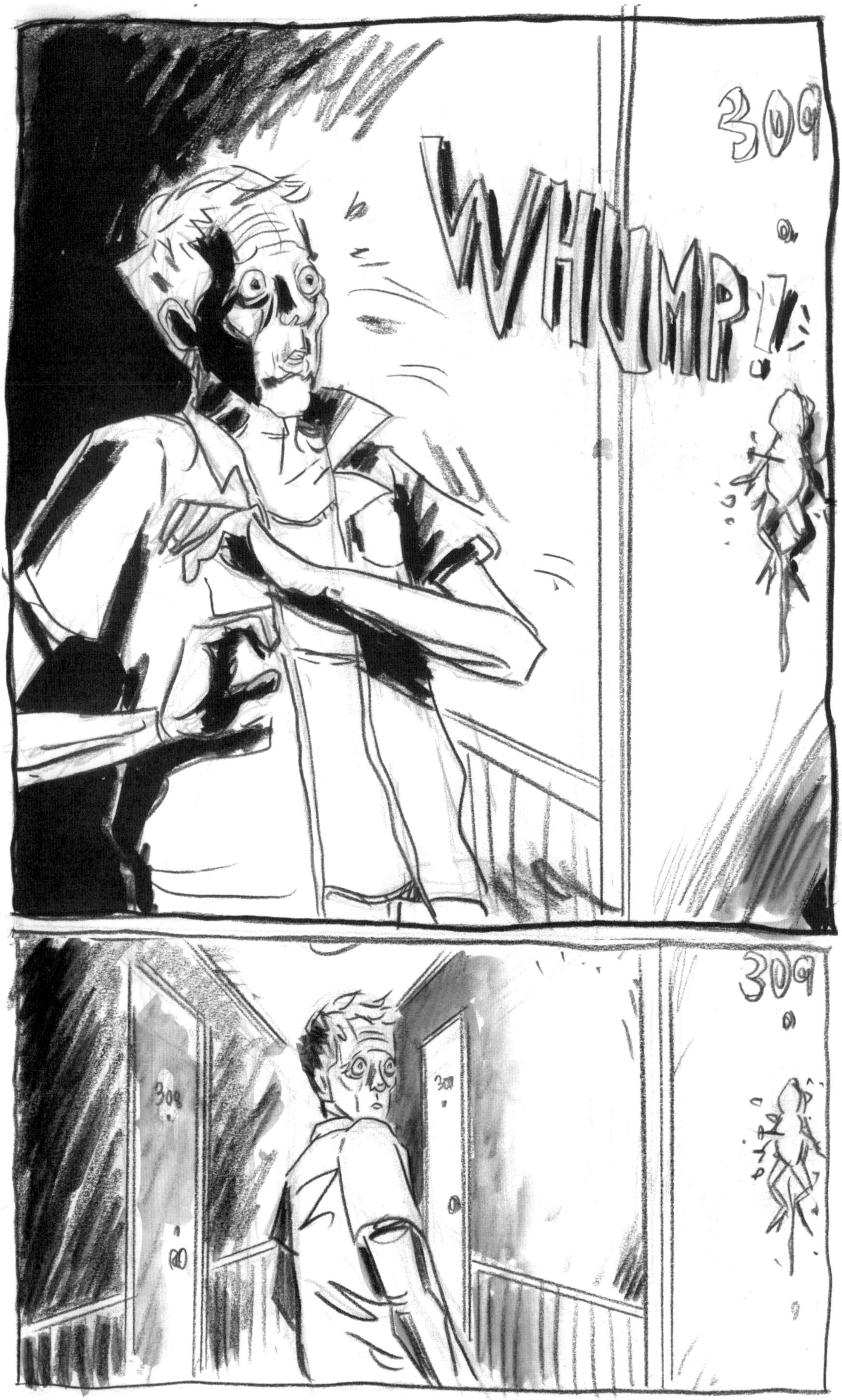
309
WHUMP!
309
308
309

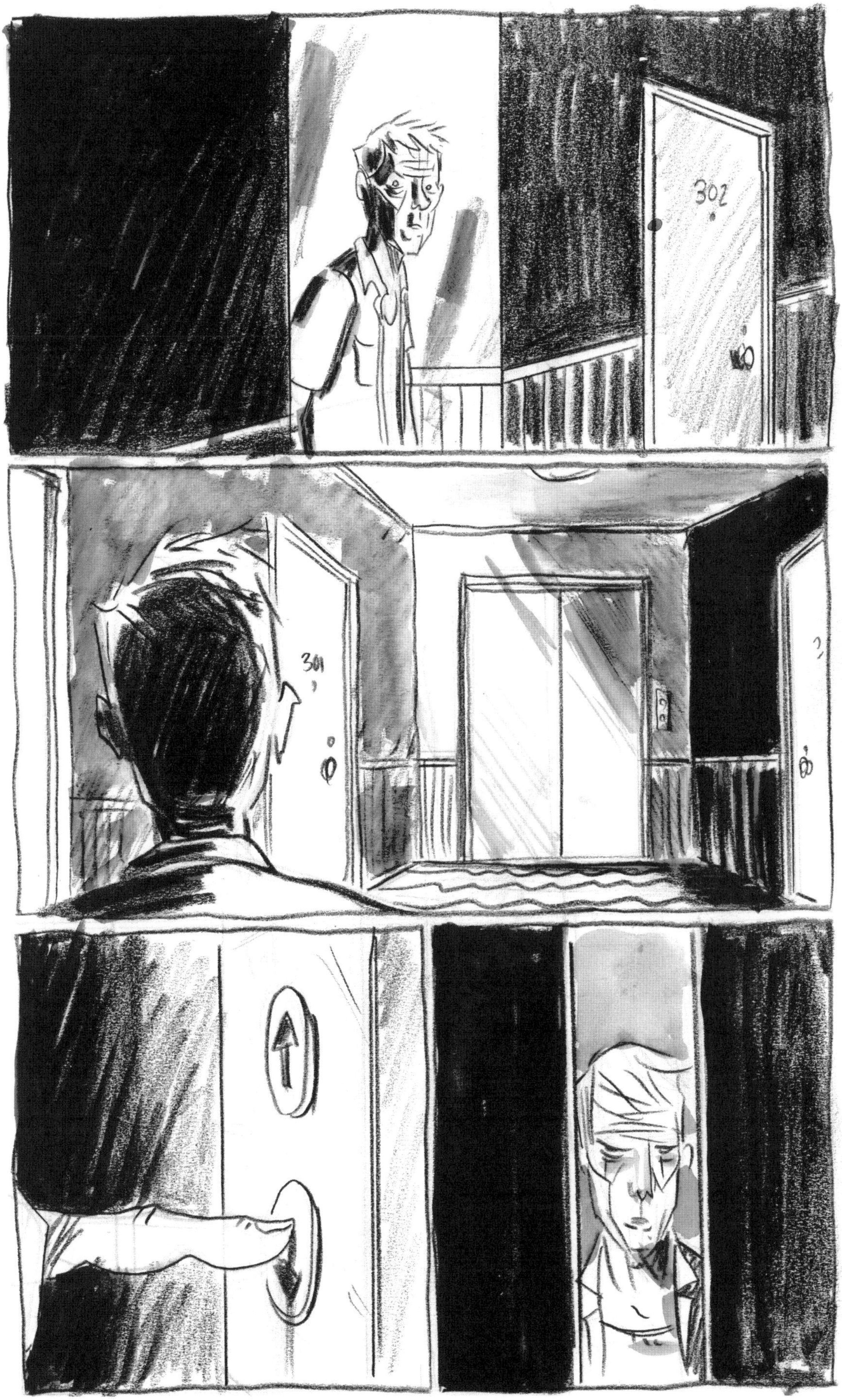
302
301

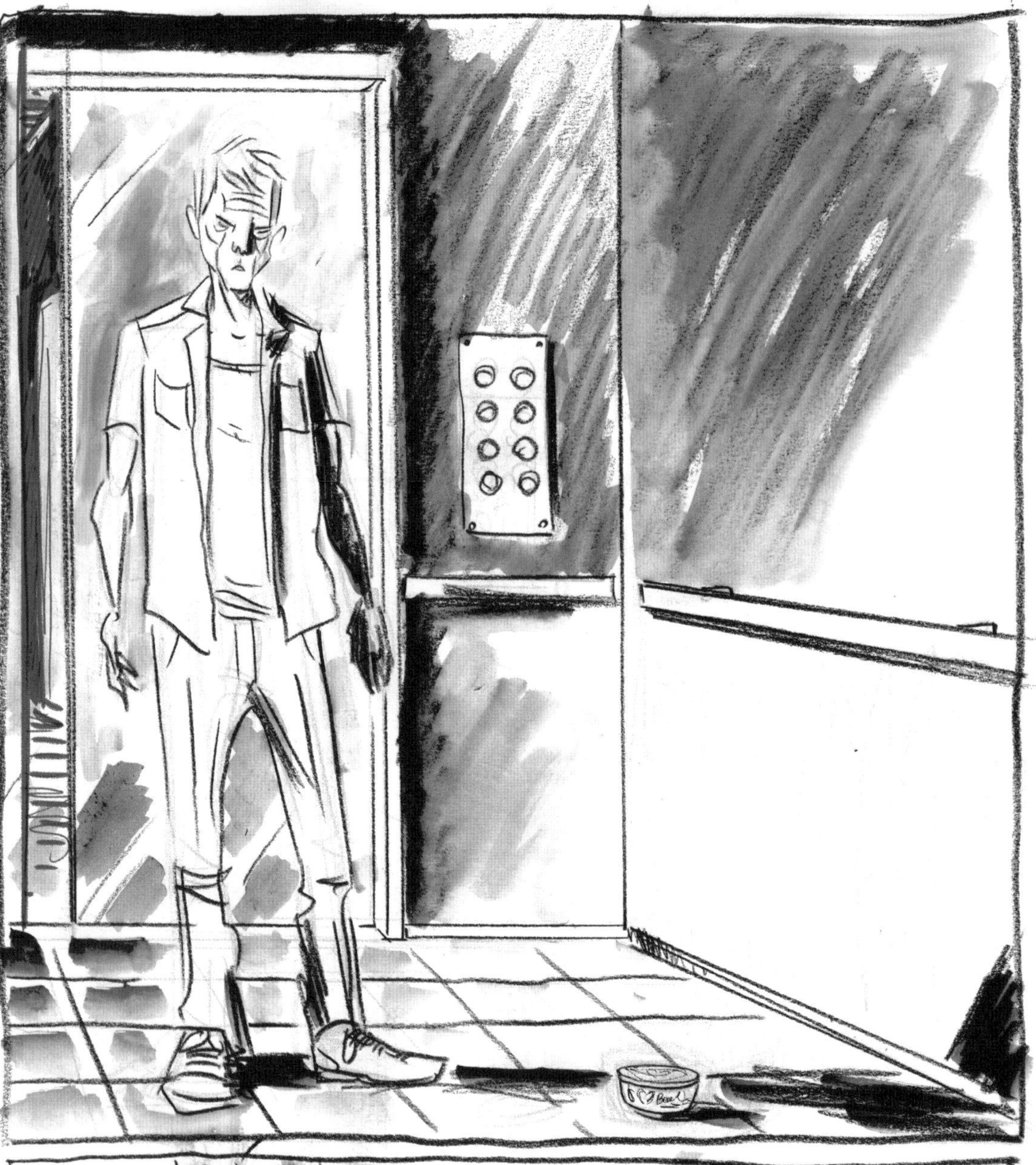

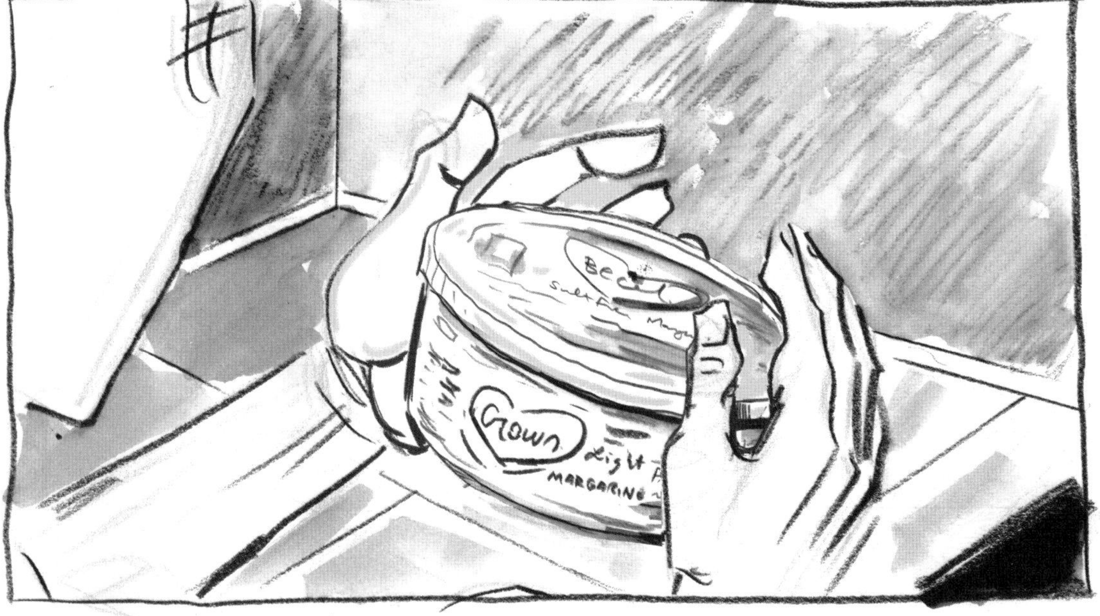
Crown
MARGARINE

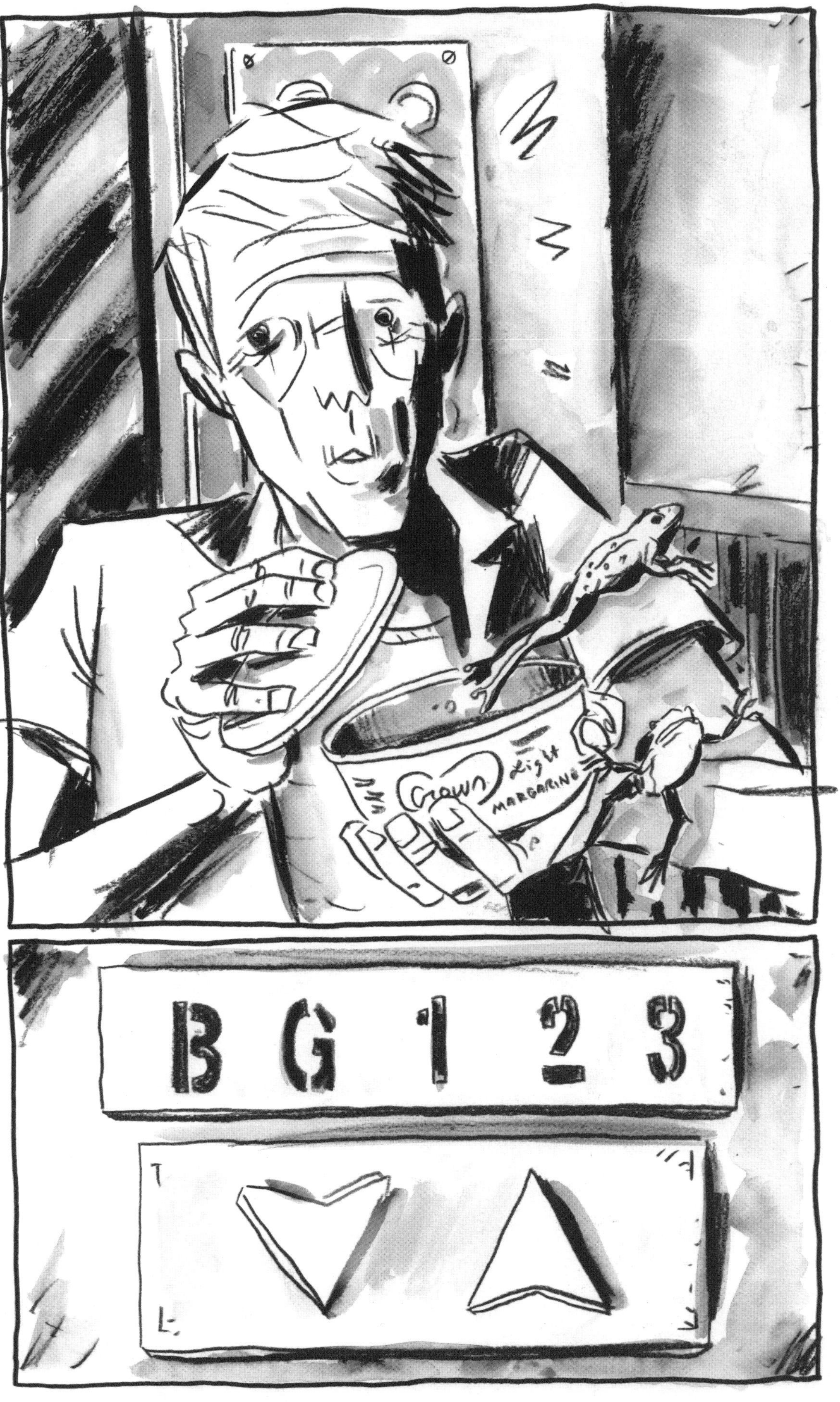
Crown Light
MARGARINE
BG 1 2 3

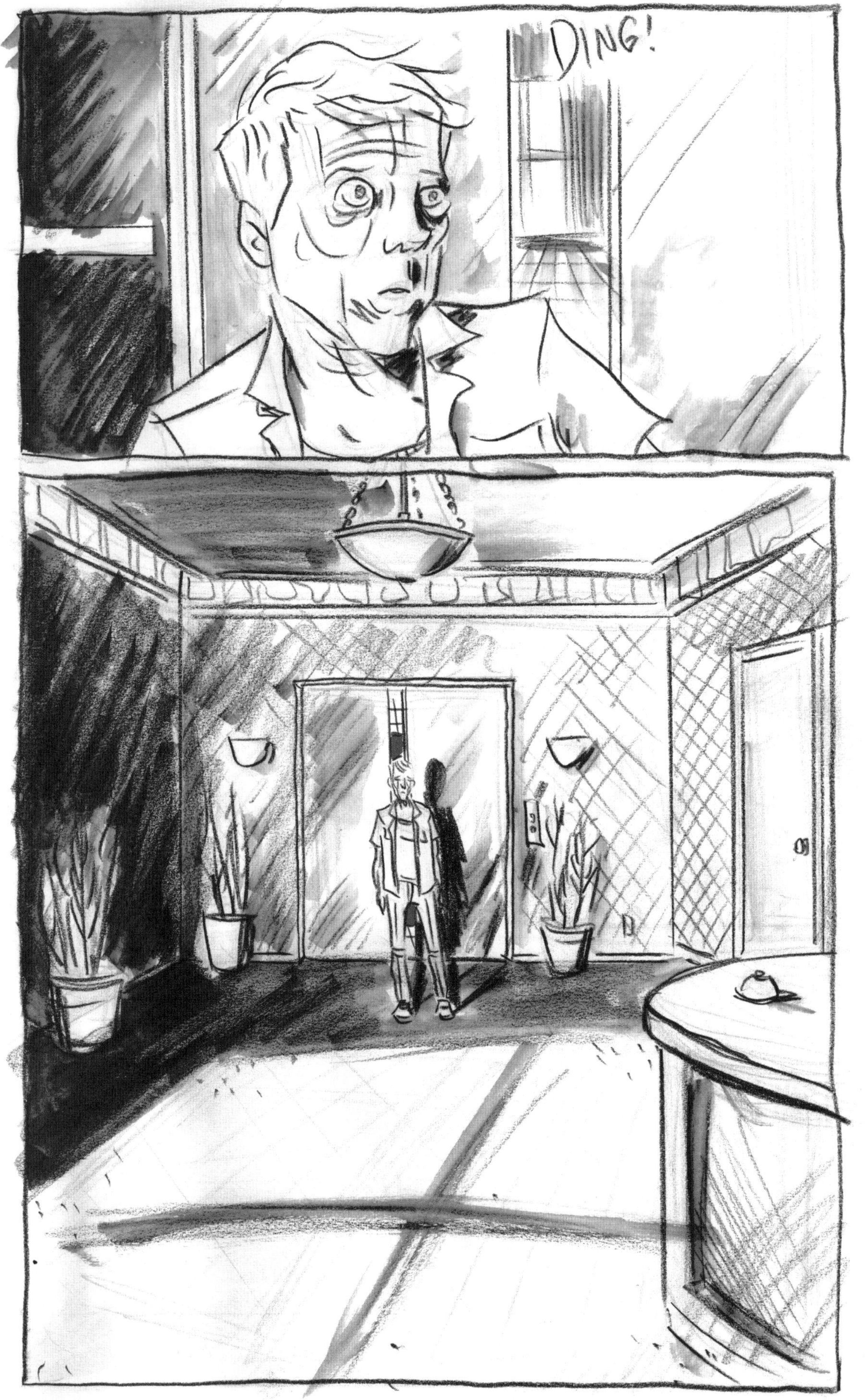
DING!

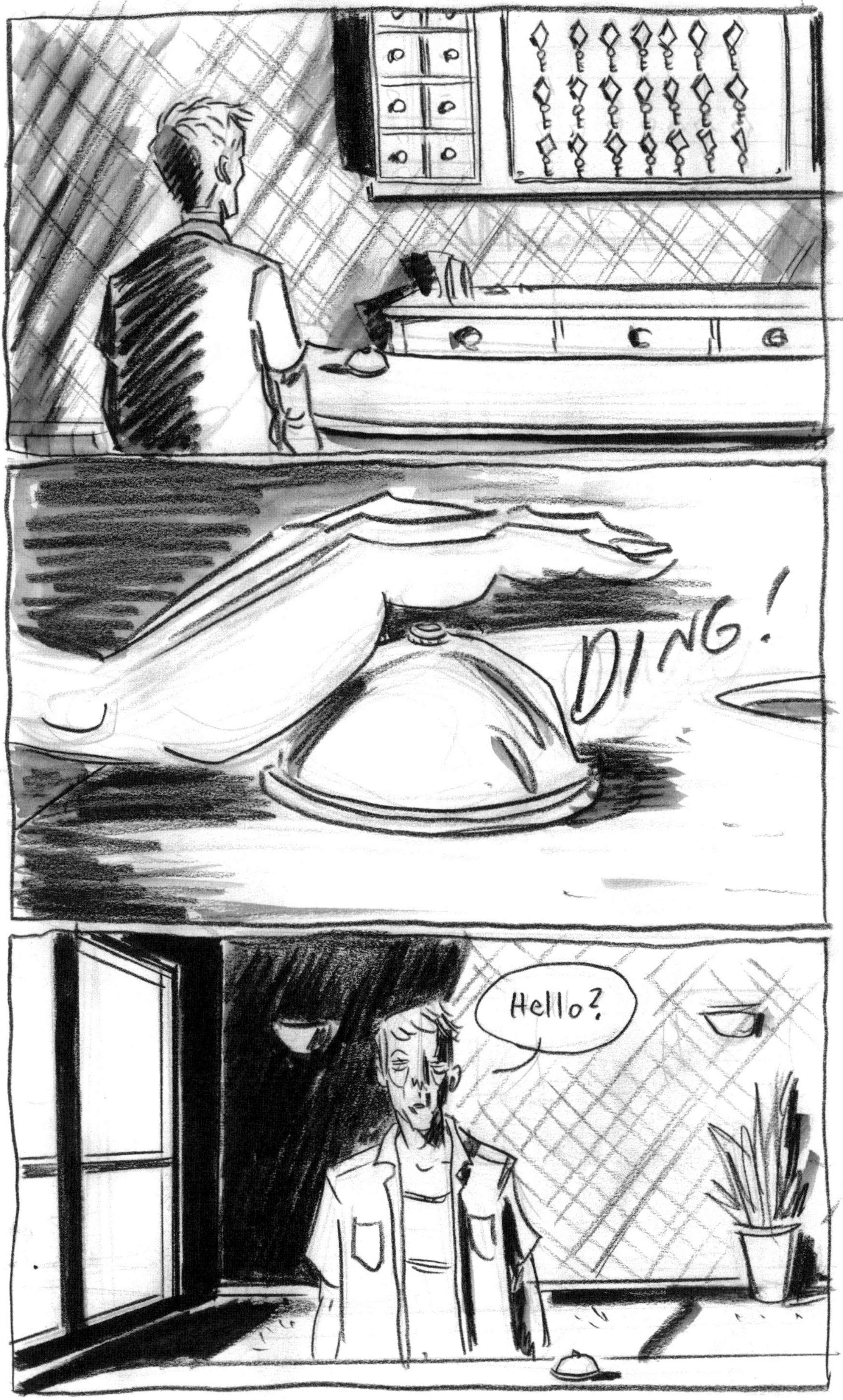
DING!
Hello?

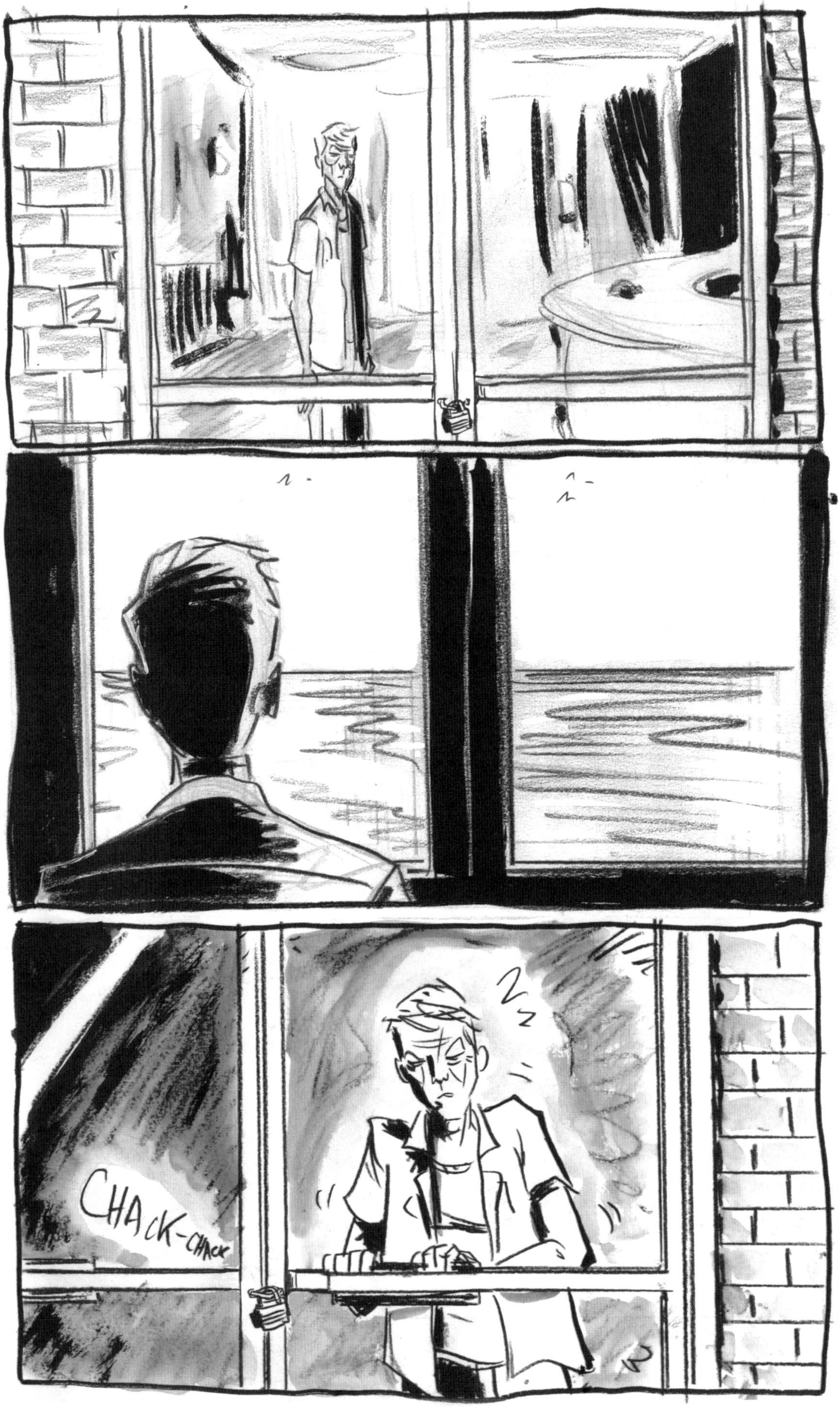
CHACK-CHACK

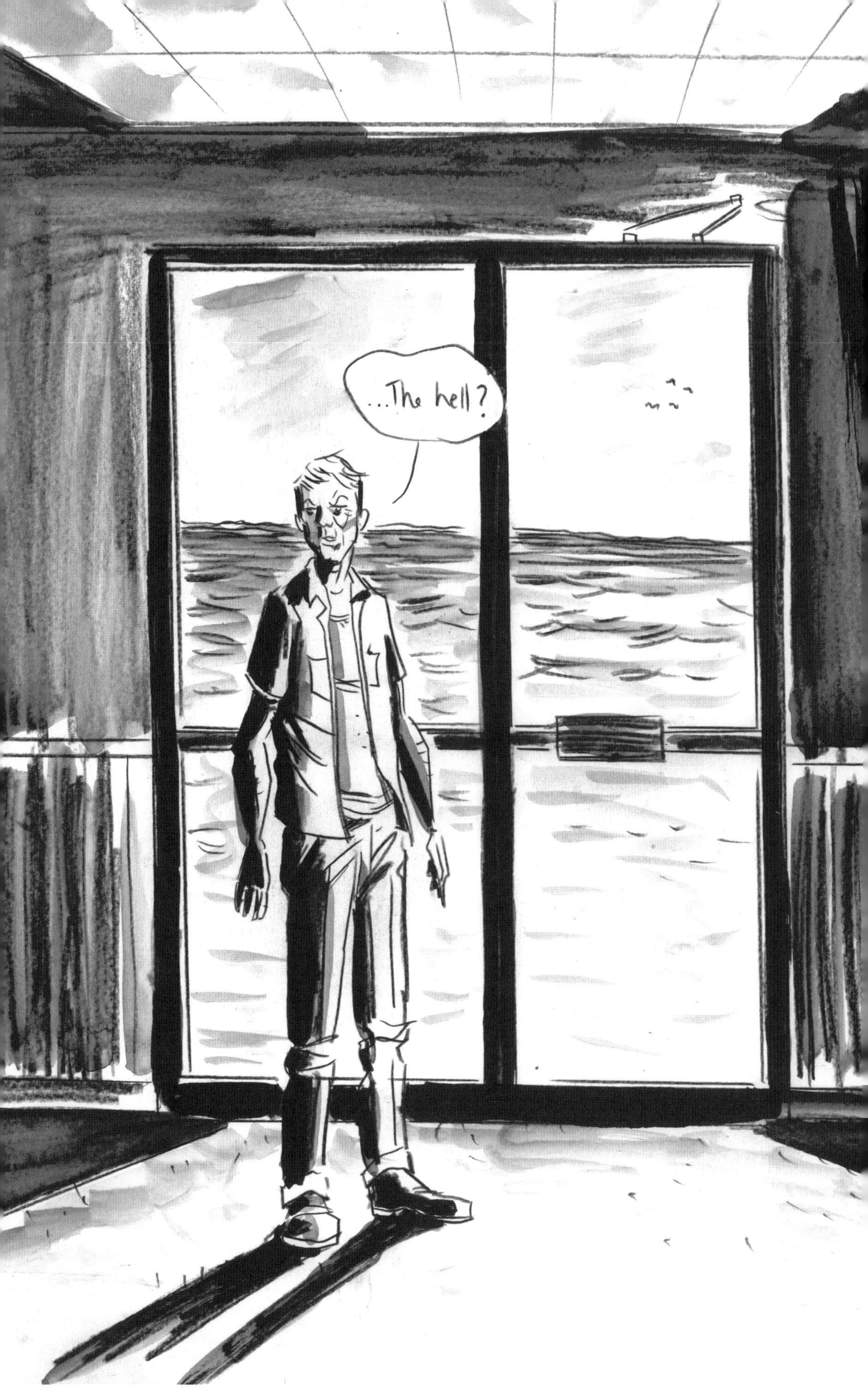
...The hell?

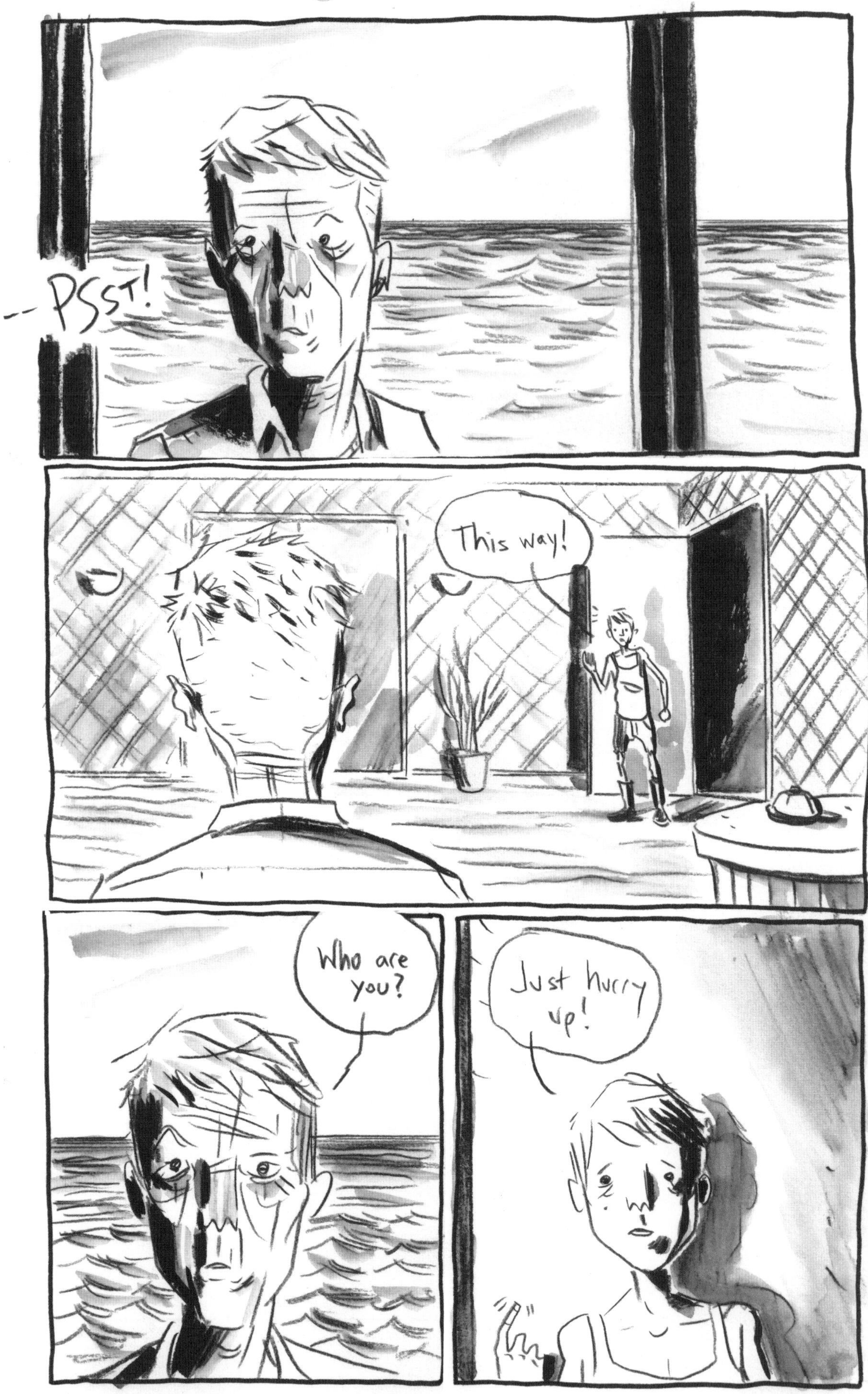
--PSST!
This way!
Who are you?
Just hurry up!

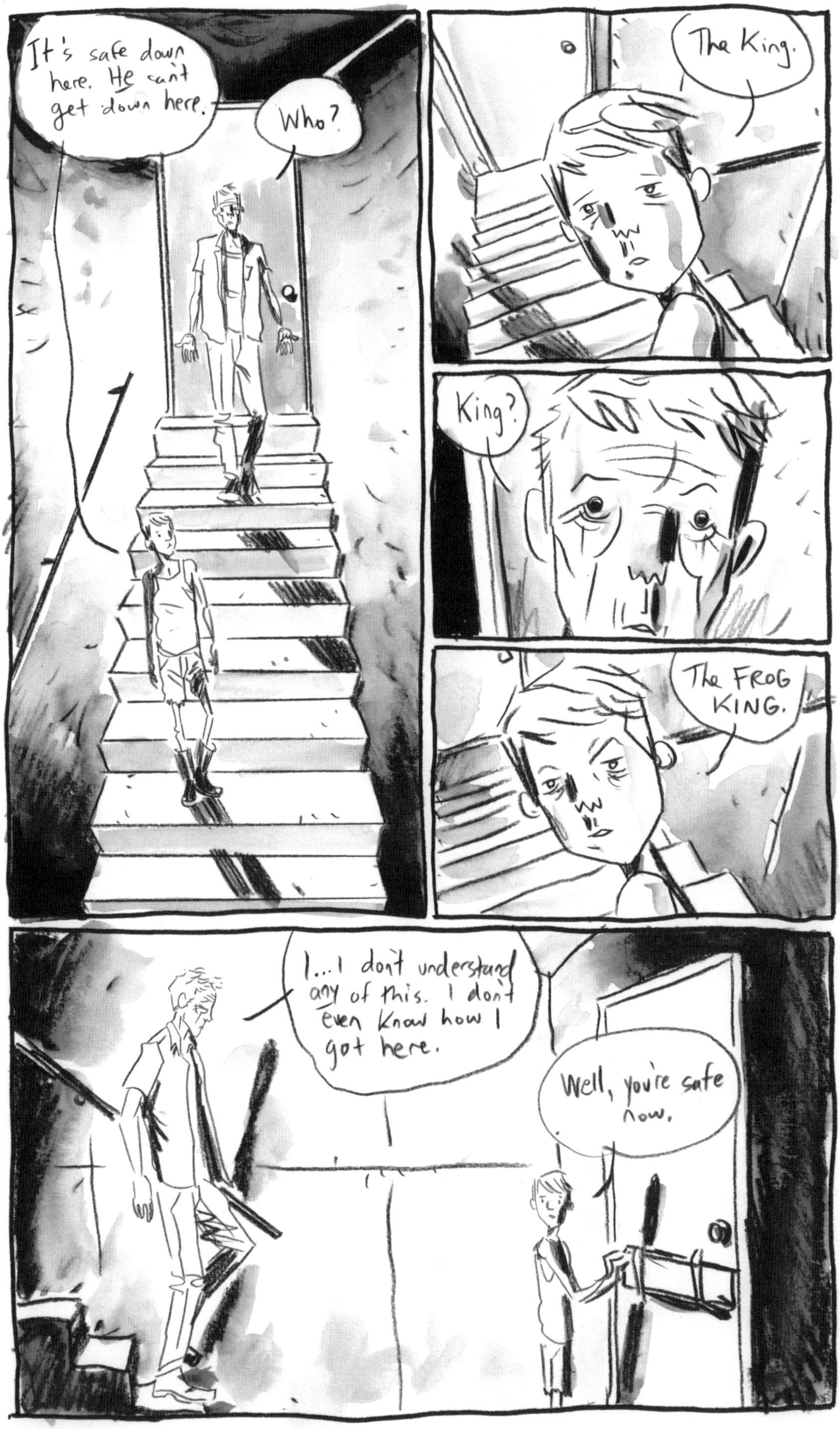
It's safe down here. He can't get down here.
Who?
The King.
King?
The FROG KING.
I... I don't understand any of this. I don't even know how I got here.
Well, you're safe now.

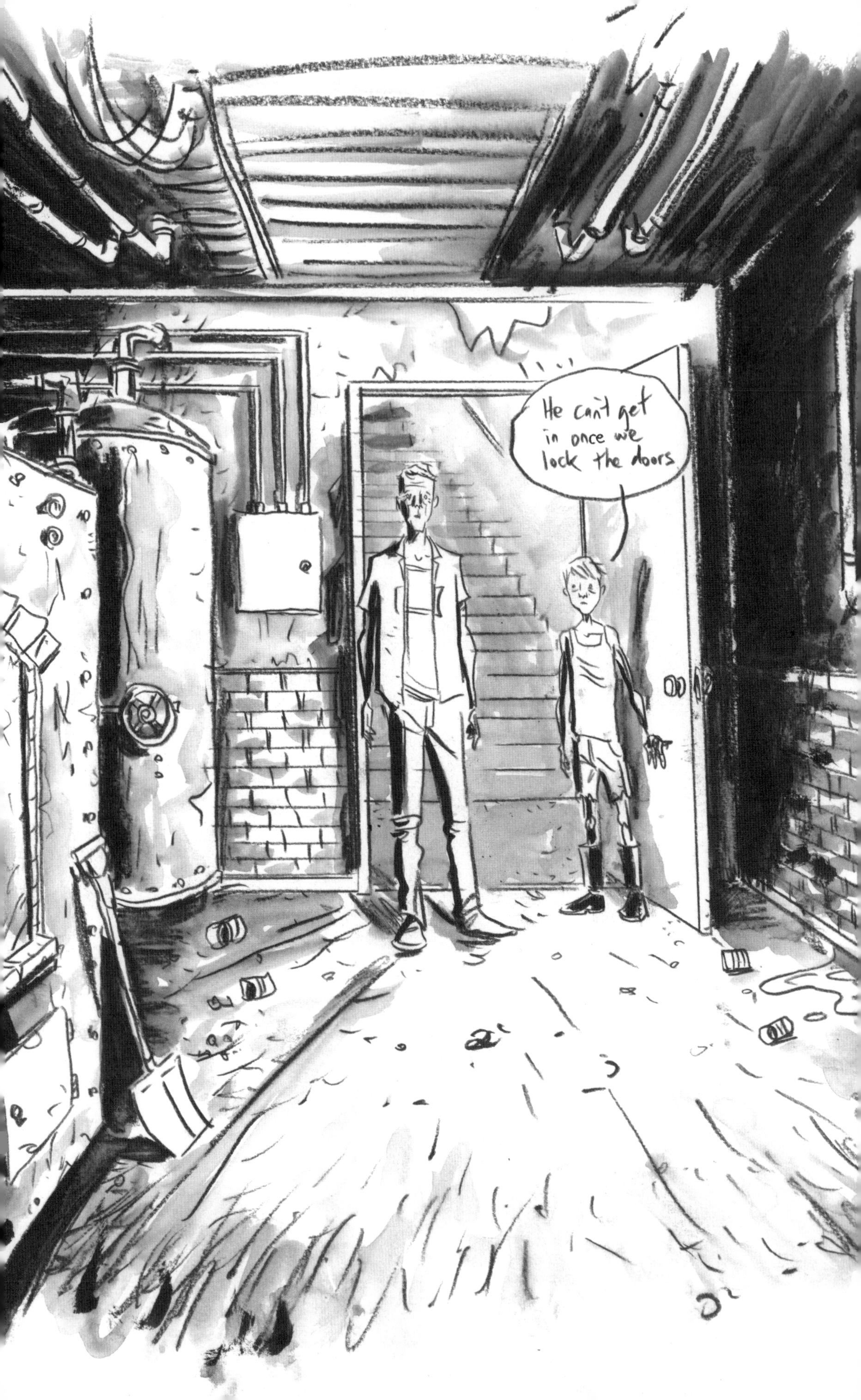
He can't get in once we lock the doors

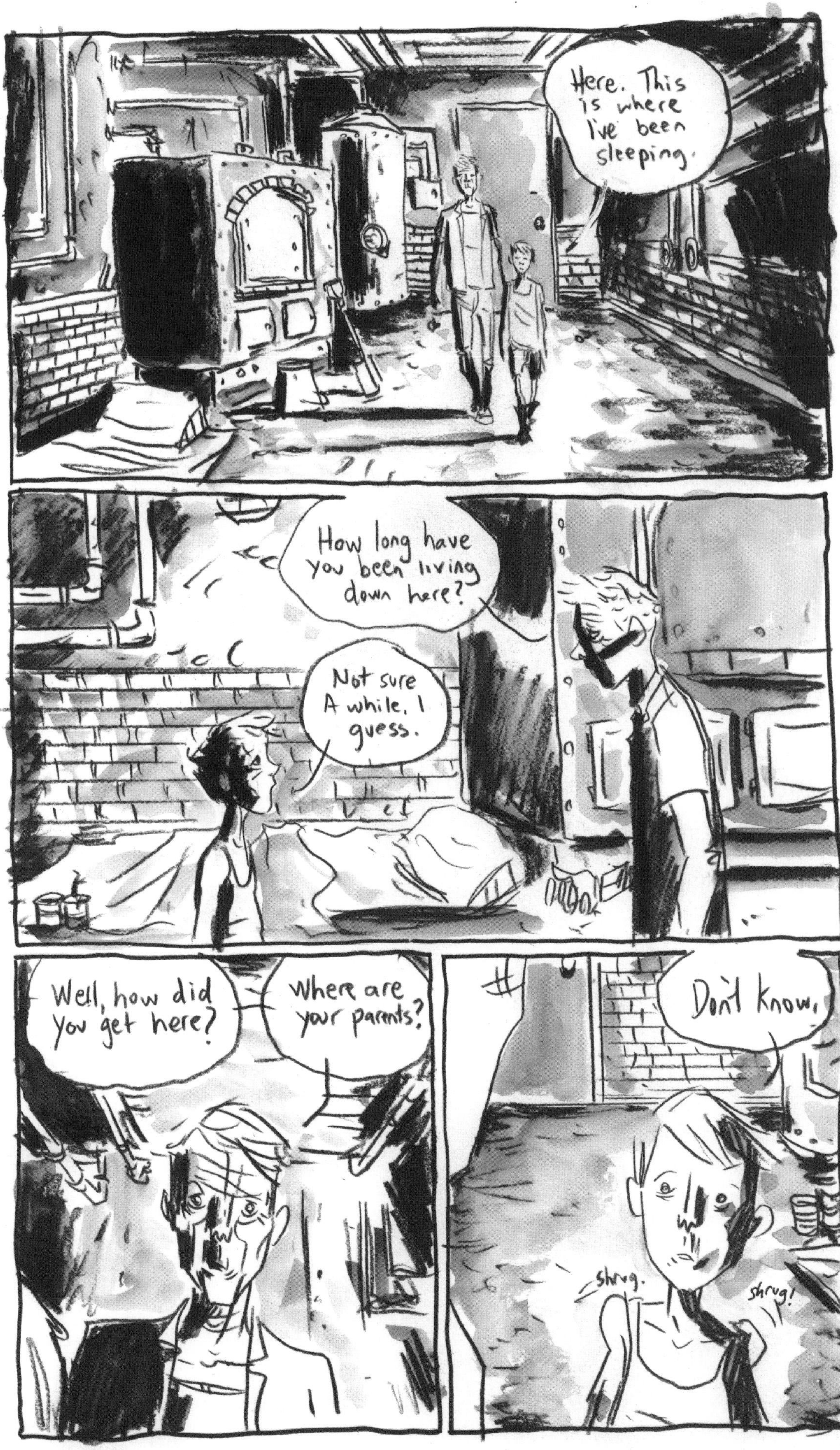
Here. This is where I've been sleeping.
How long have you been living down here?
Not sure A while, I guess.
Well, how did you get here?
Where are your parents?
Don't know.
shrug.
shrug!

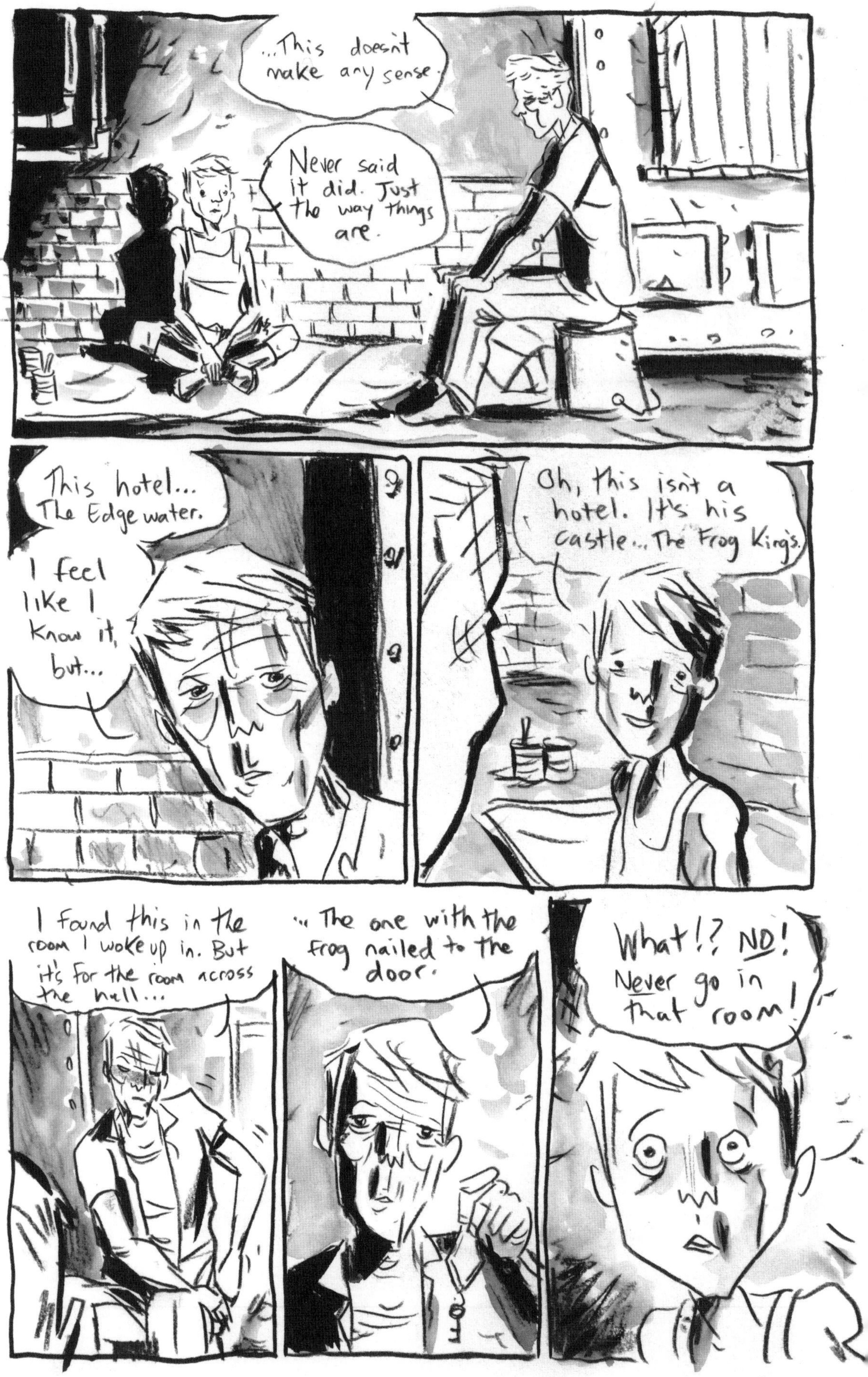
...This doesn't make any sense.
Never said it did. Just the way things are.
This hotel... The Edgewater.
I feel like I know it, but...
Oh, this isn't a hotel. It's his castle... The Frog King's.
I found this in the room I woke up in. But it's for the room across the hall...
... The one with the frog nailed to the door.
What!? NO! Never go in that room!

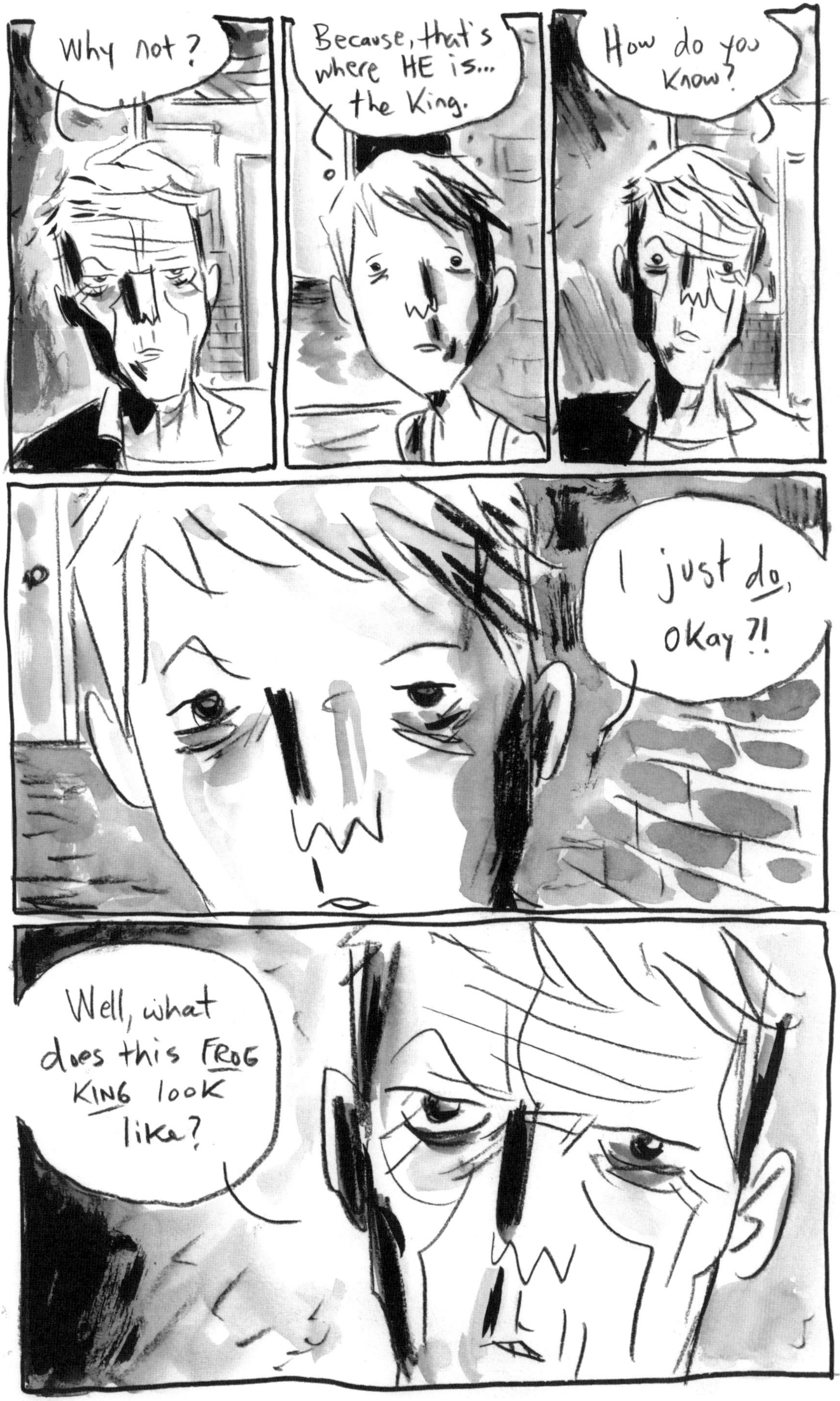
Why not?
Because, that's where HE is... the King.
How do you know?
I just do, okay?!
Well, what does this FROG KING look like?

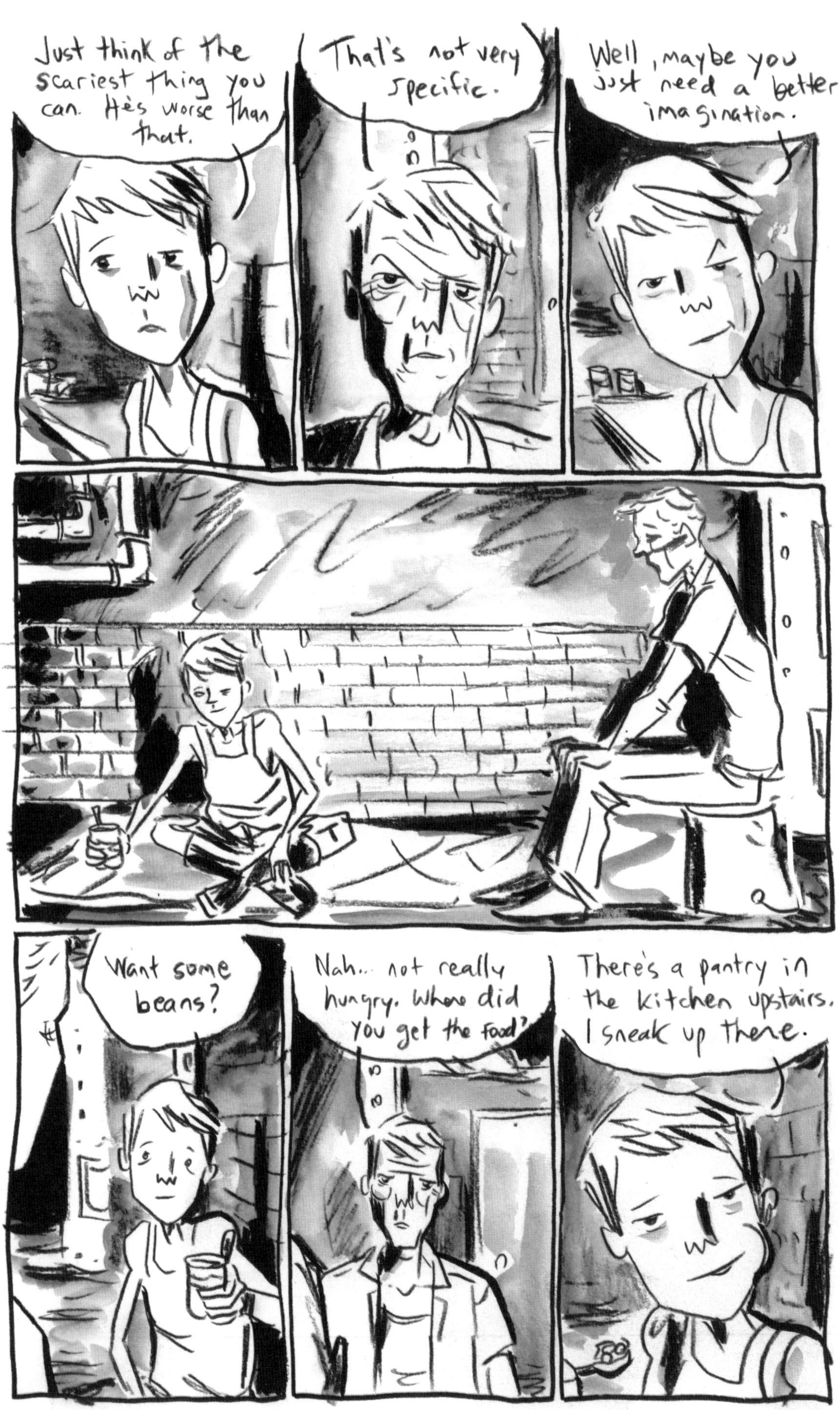
Just think of the scariest thing you can. He's worse than that.
That's not very specific.
Well, maybe you just need a better imagination.
Want some beans?
Nah... not really hungry. Where did you get the food?
There's a pantry in the kitchen upstairs. I sneak up there.

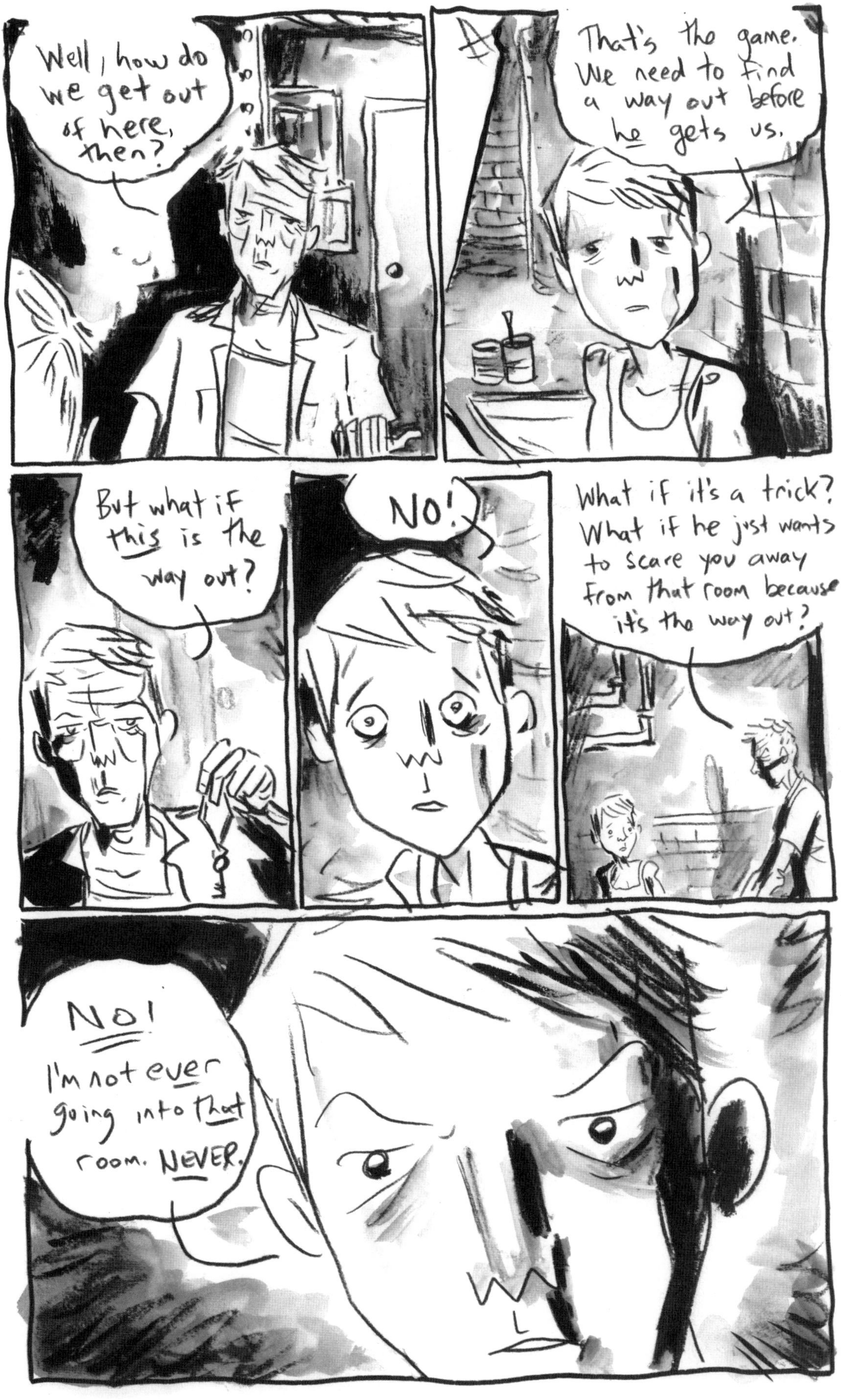
Well, how do we get out of here, then?
That's the game. We need to find a way out before he gets us.
But what if this is the way out?
NO!
What if it's a trick? What if he just wants to scare you away from that room because it's the way out?
NO! I'm not ever going into that room. NEVER.

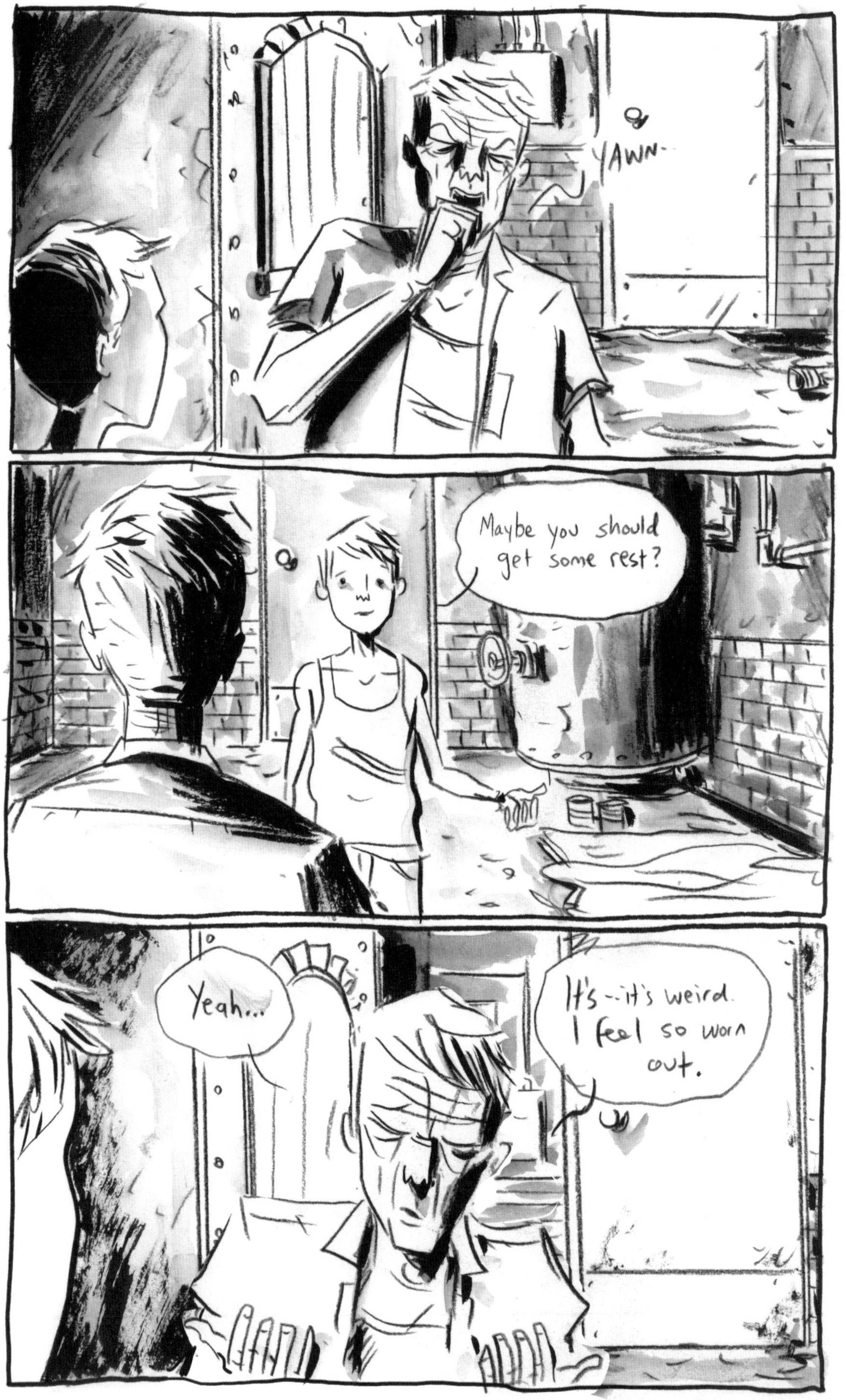
YAWN-
Maybe you should get some rest?
Yeah...
It's--it's weird. I feel so worn out.

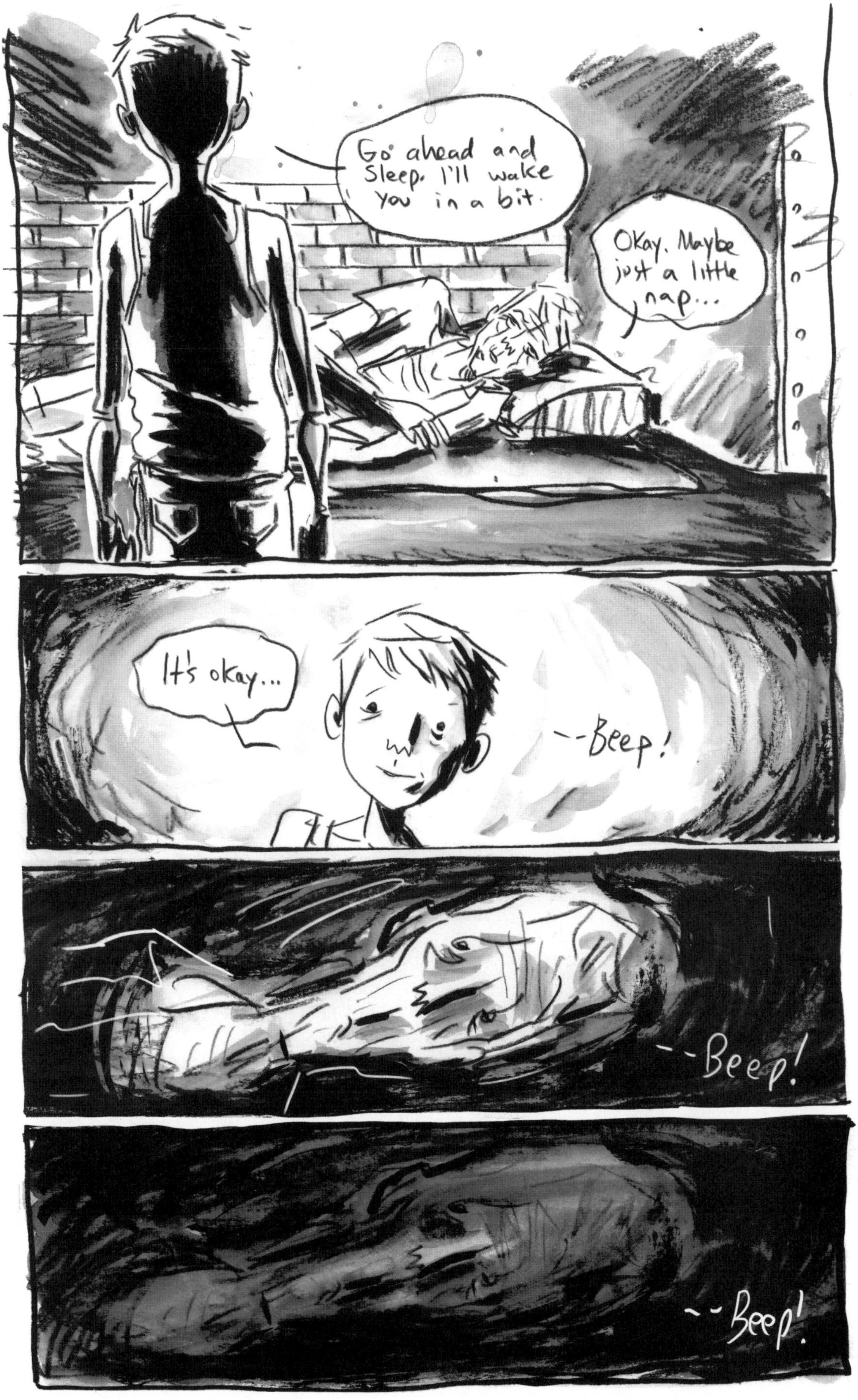
Go ahead and Sleep. I'll wake you in a bit.
Okay. Maybe just a little nap...
It's okay...
--Beep!
--Beep!
--Beep!

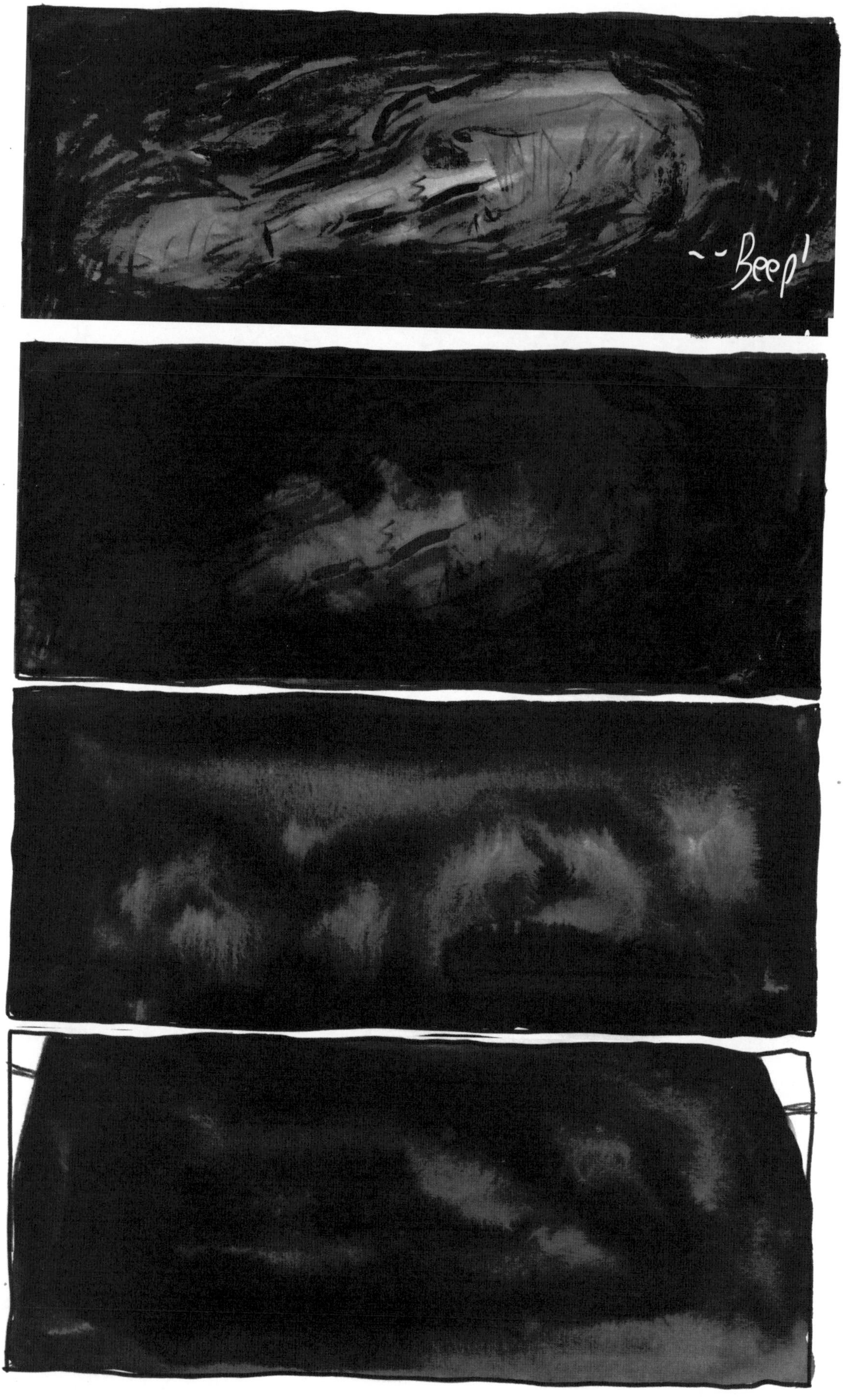

--Beep'

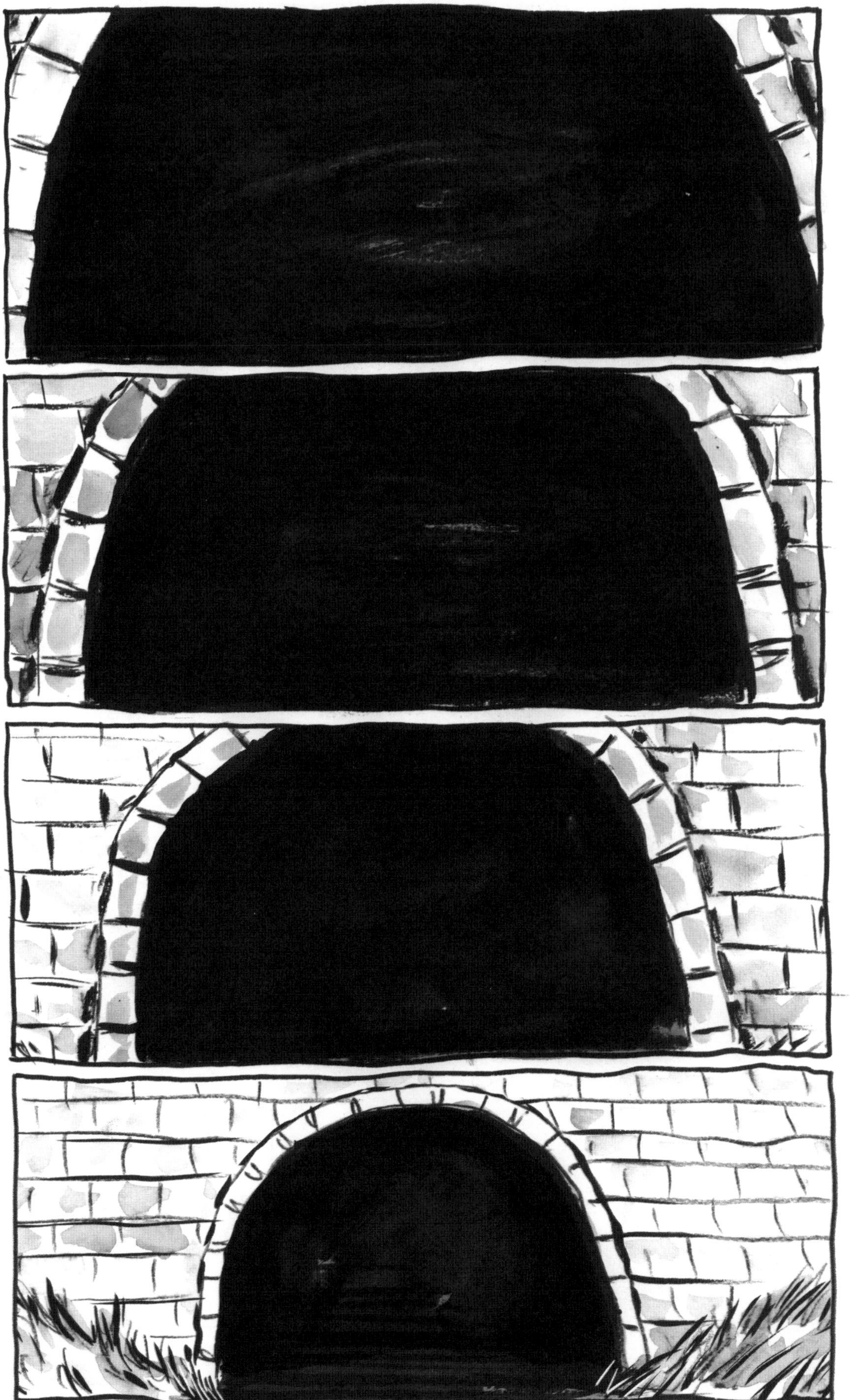

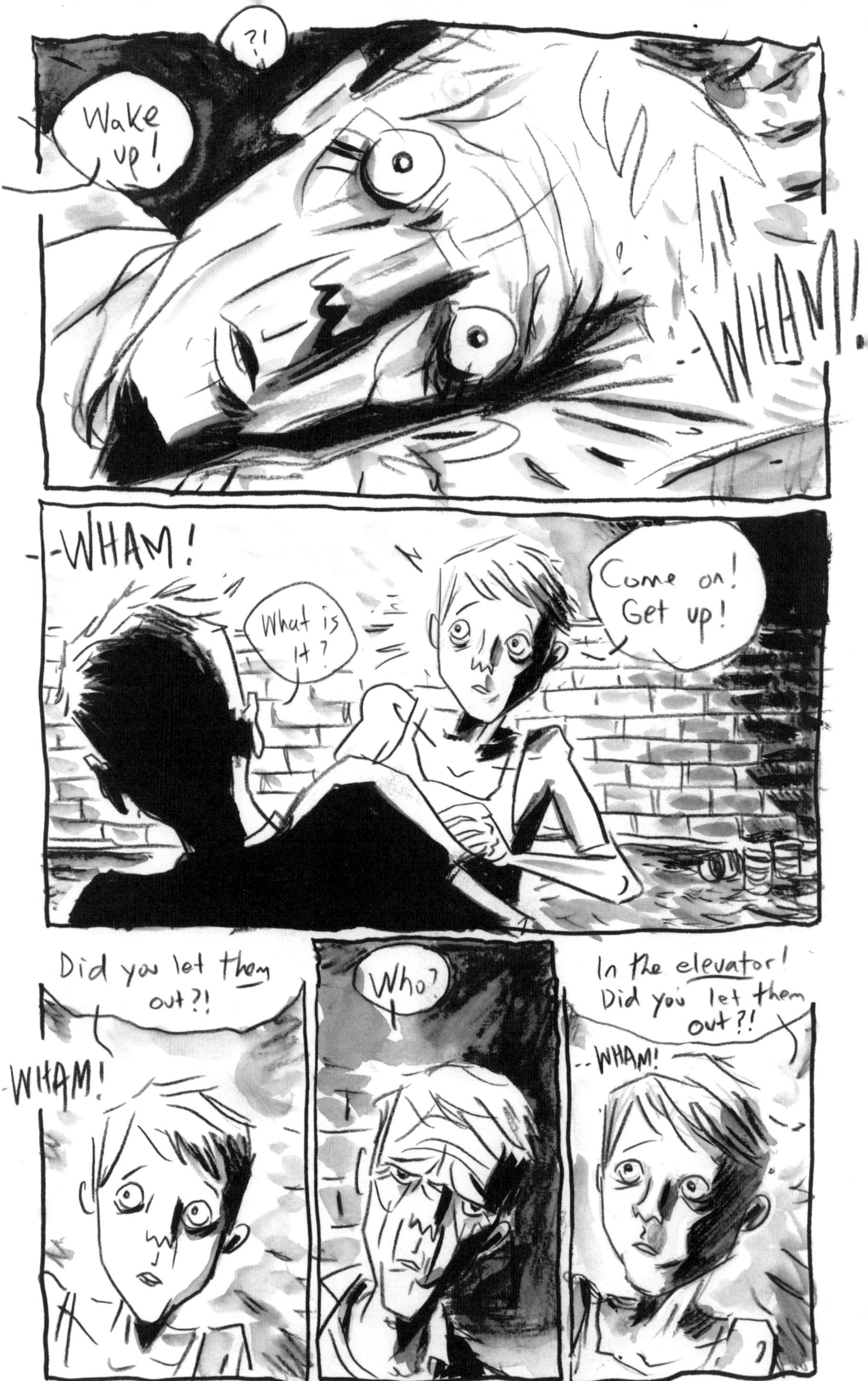

?!
Wake up!
WHAM!
WHAM!
What is it?
Come on! Get up!
Did you let them out?!
WHAM!
Who?
In the elevator! Did you let them out?!
WHAM!

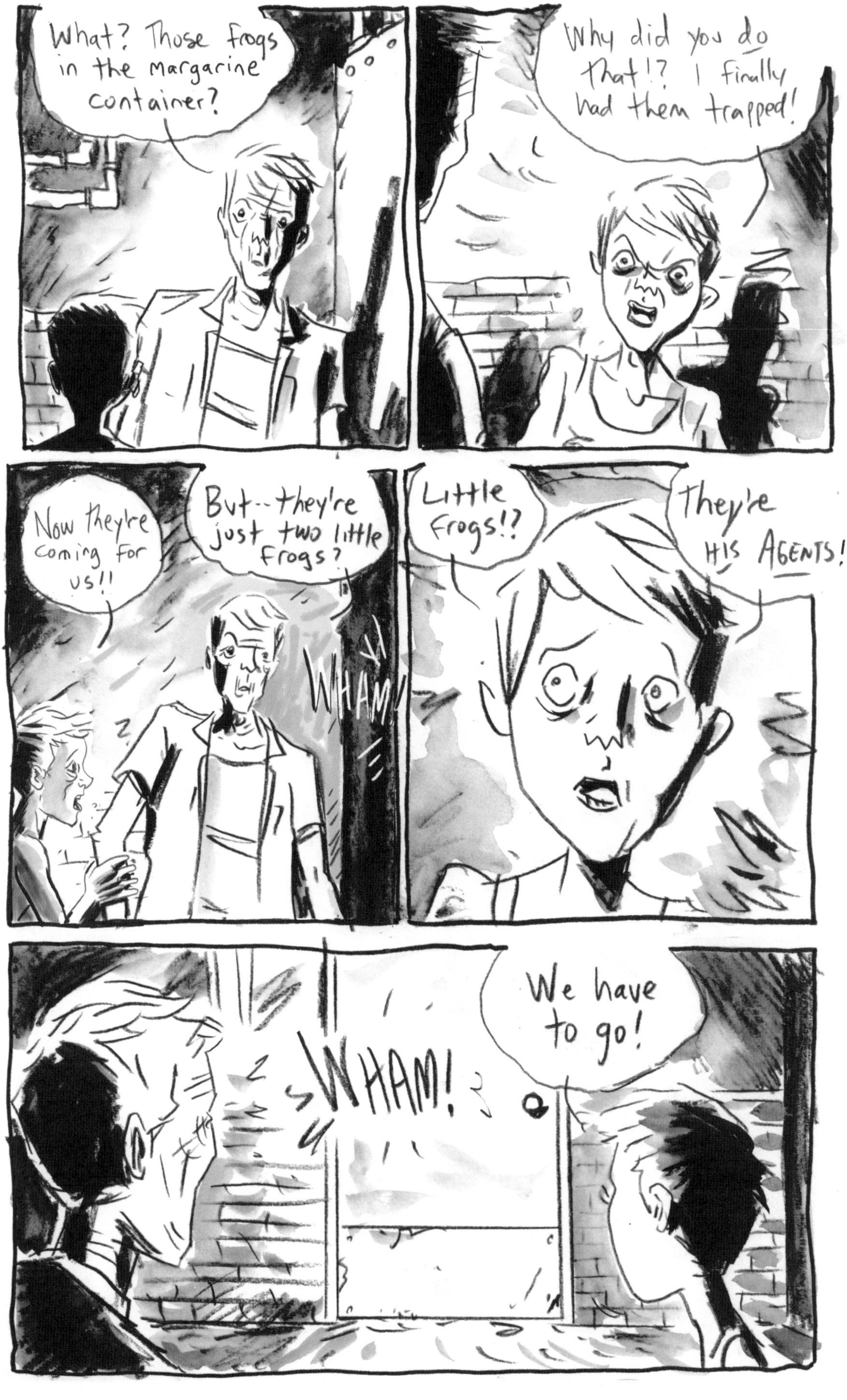
What? Those frogs in the margarine container?
Why did you do that!? I finally had them trapped!
Now they're coming for us!!
But...they're just two little frogs?
WHAM!
Little frogs!?
They're HIS AGENTS!
WHAM!
We have to go!

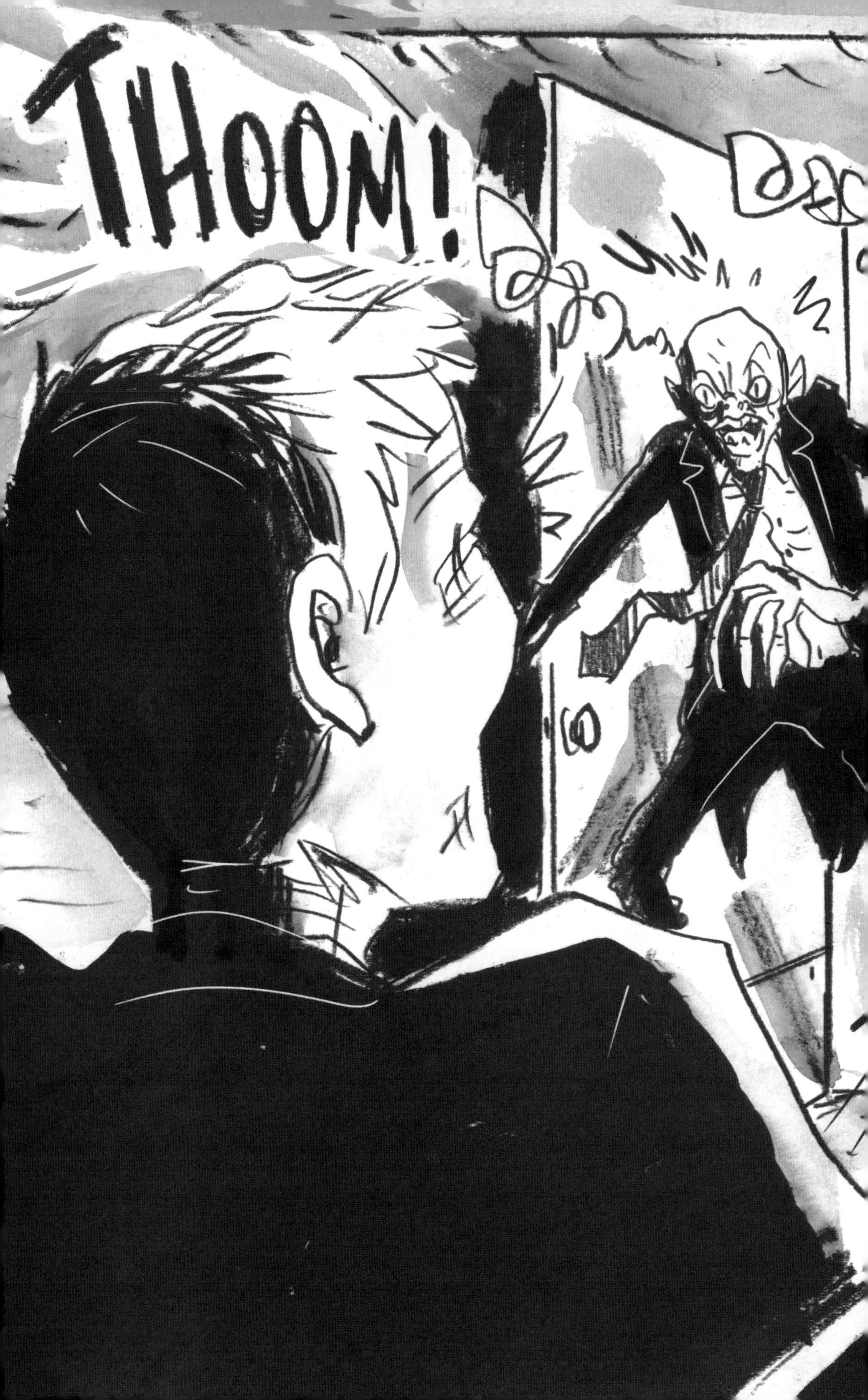
THOOM!

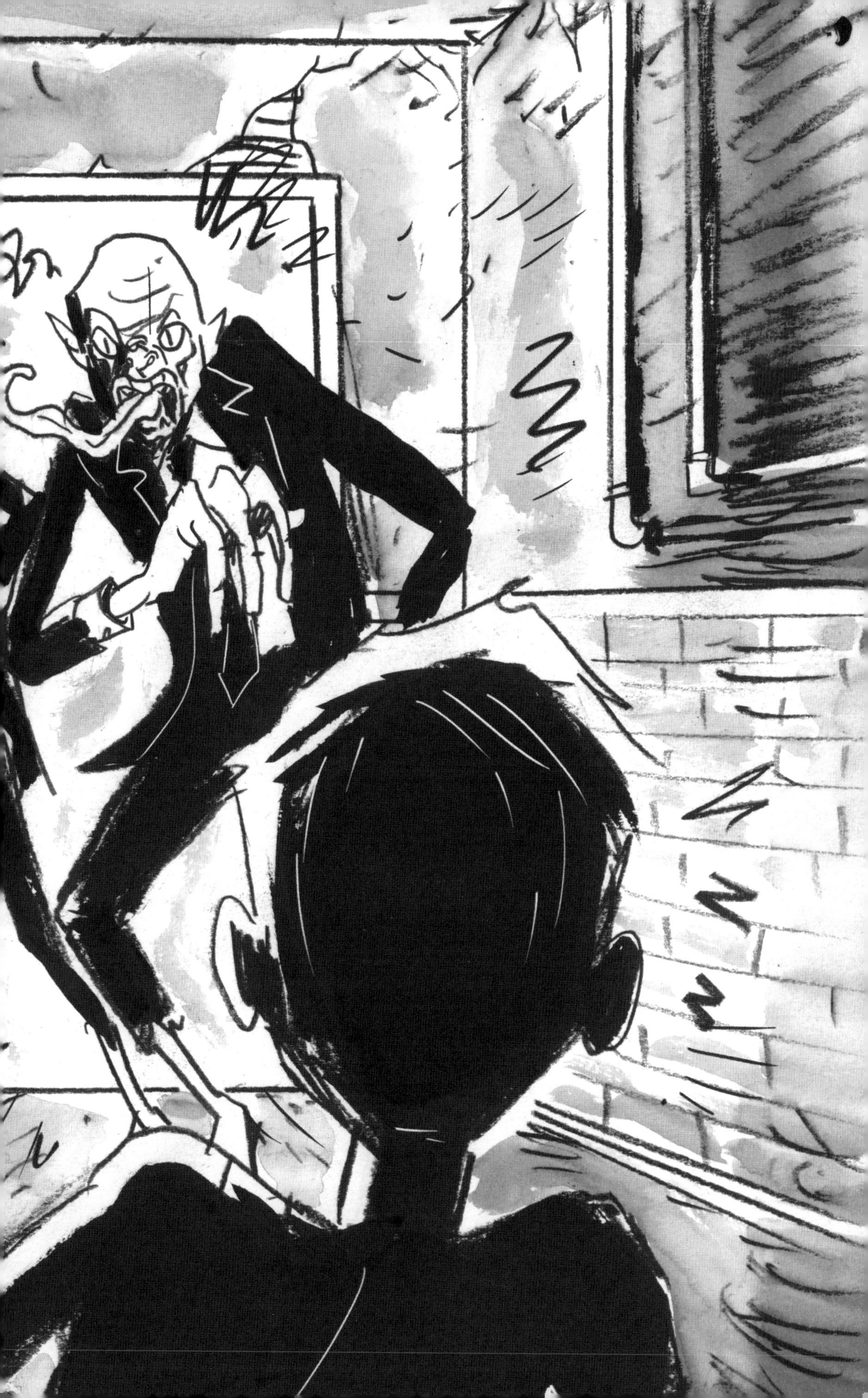

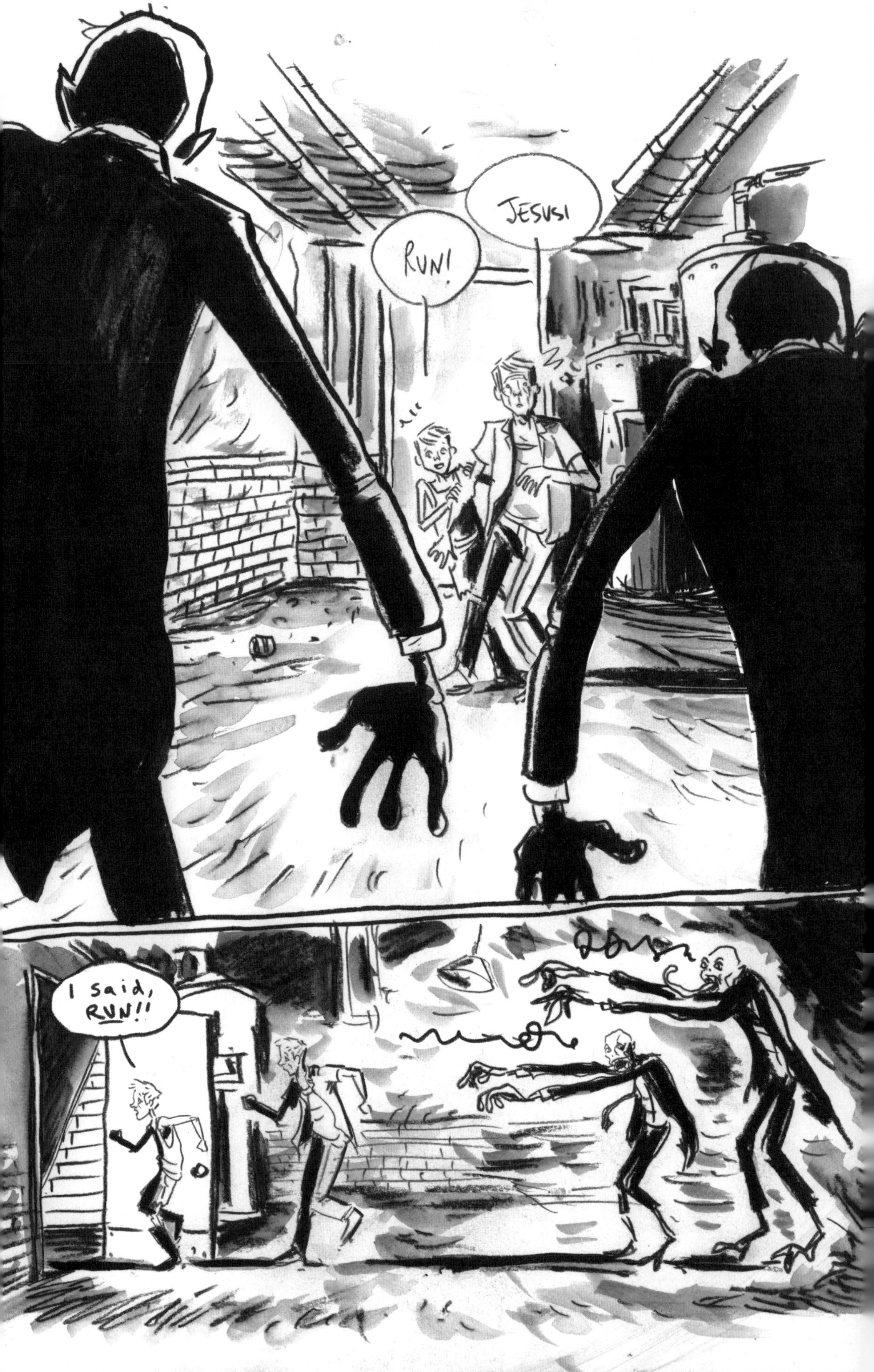
RUN!
JESUS!
I said, RUN!!

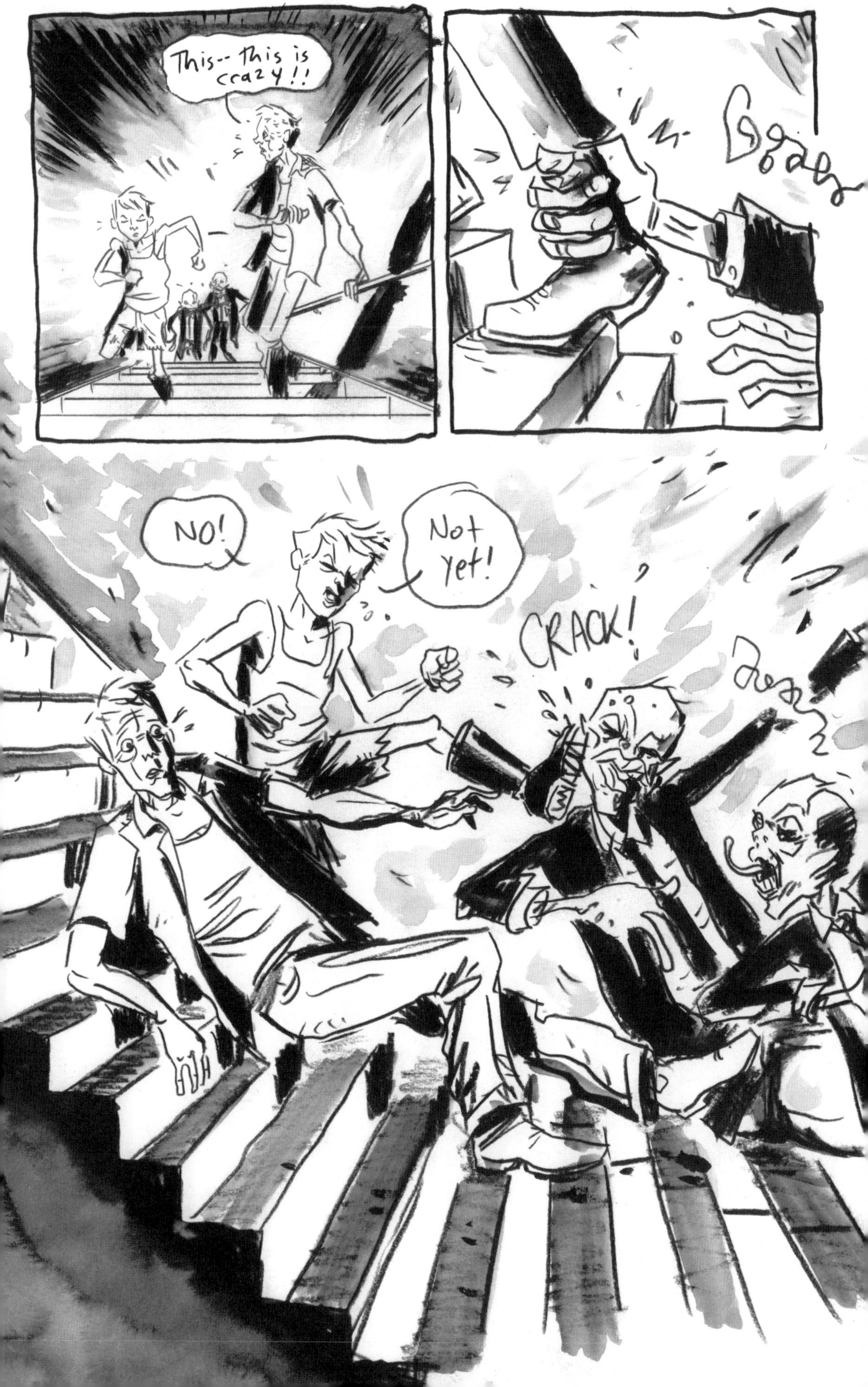
This-- this is crazy!!
NO!
Not yet!
CRACK!

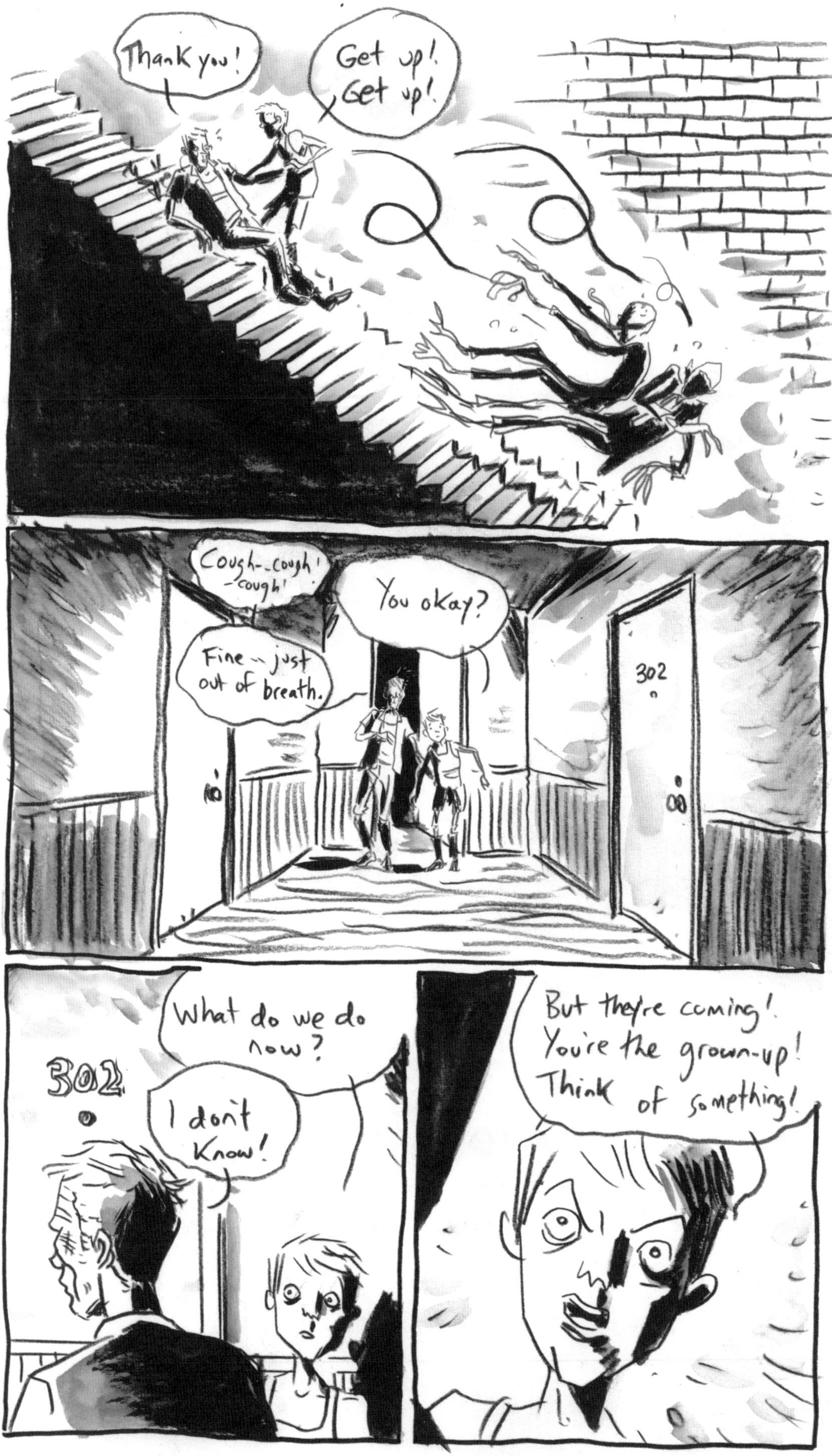
Thank you!
Get up! Get up!
Cough--cough! -cough!
You okay?
Fine -- just out of breath.
302
302
What do we do now?
I don't know!
But they're coming! You're the grown-up! Think of something!

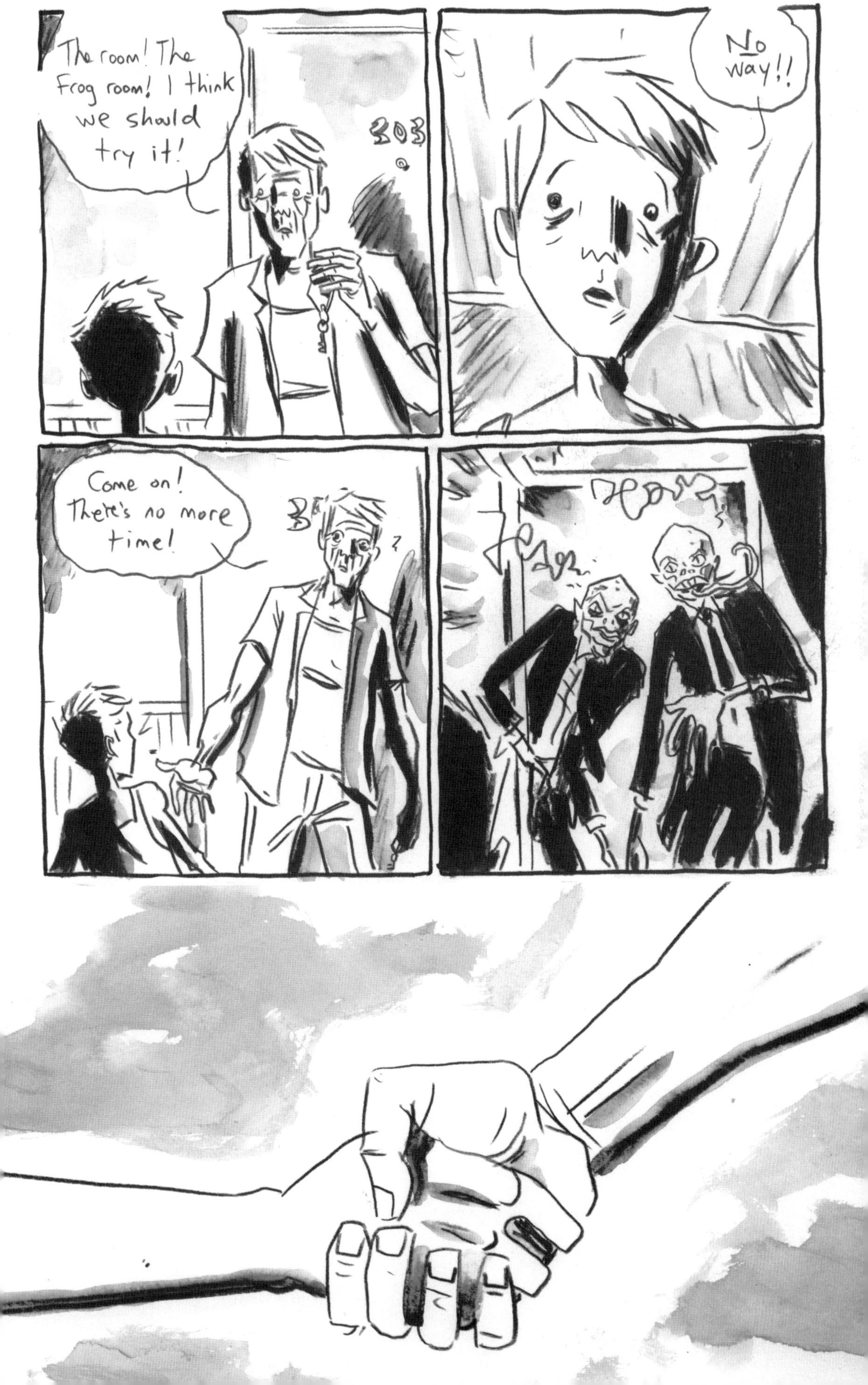
The room! The Frog room! I think we should try it!
303
No way!!
Come on! There's no more time!

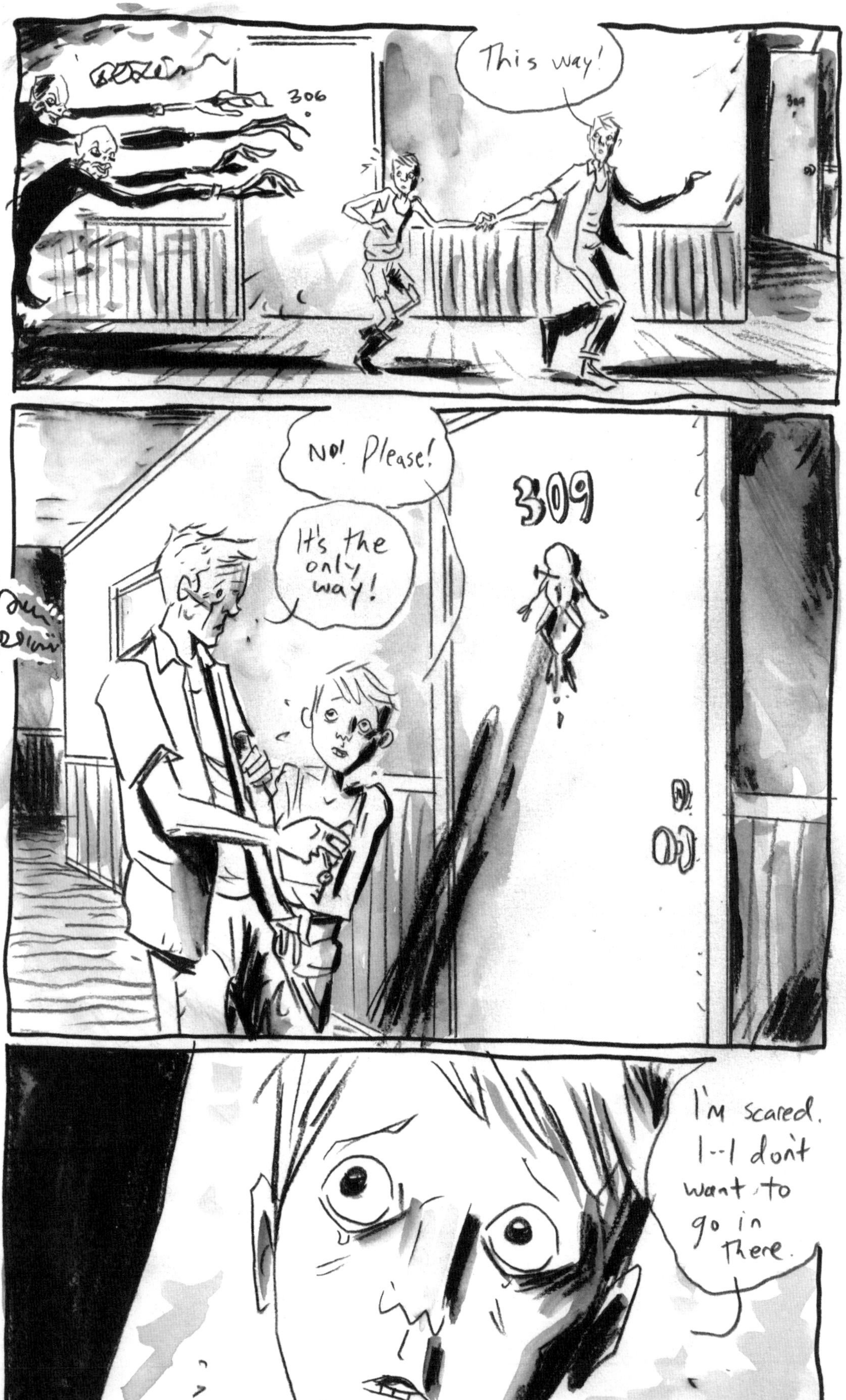
306
This way!
No! Please!
It's the only way!
309
I'm scared. I--I don't want to go in there.

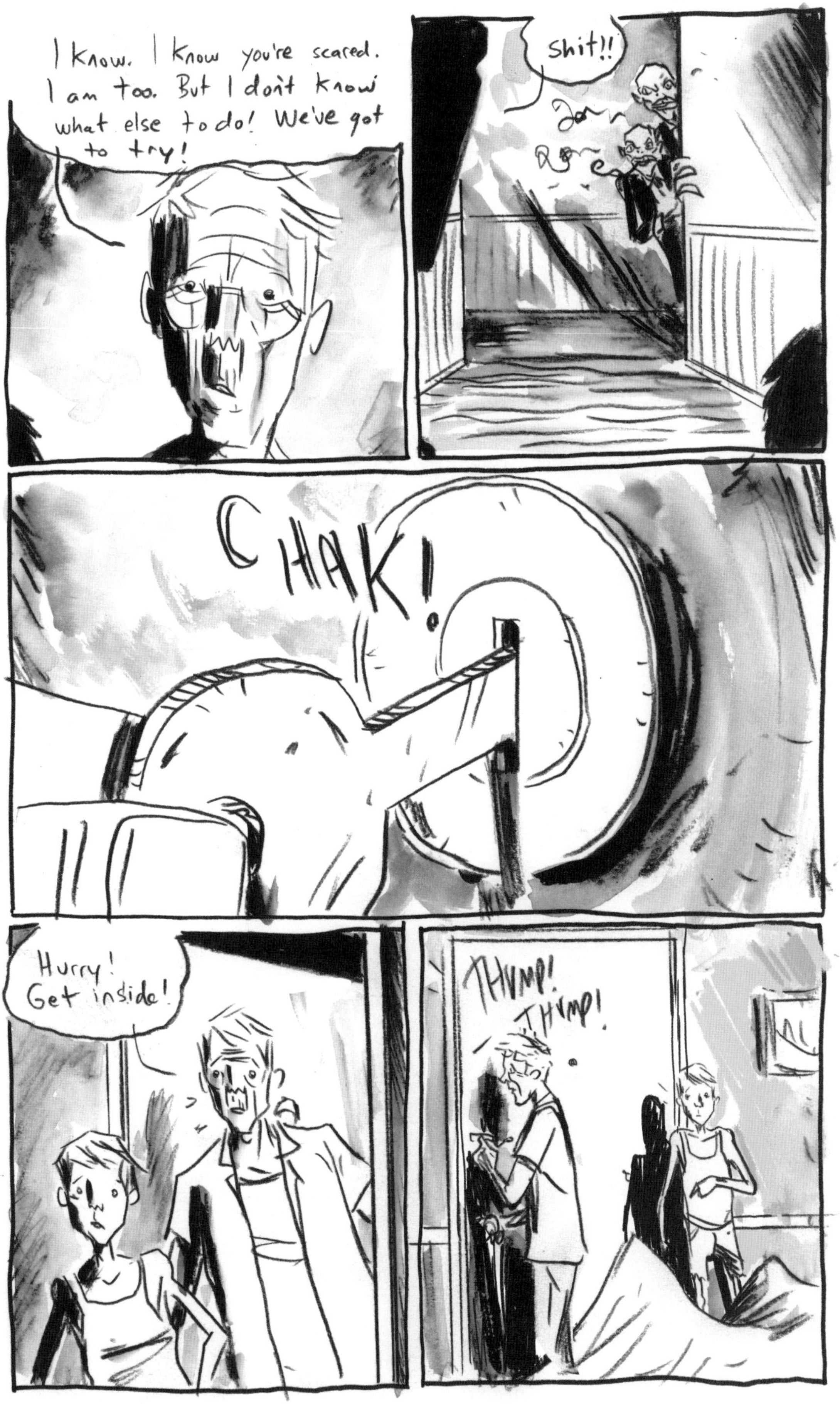
I know. I know you're scared. I am too. But I don't know what else to do! We've got to try!
Shit!!
CHAK!
Hurry! Get inside!
THUMP! THUMP!

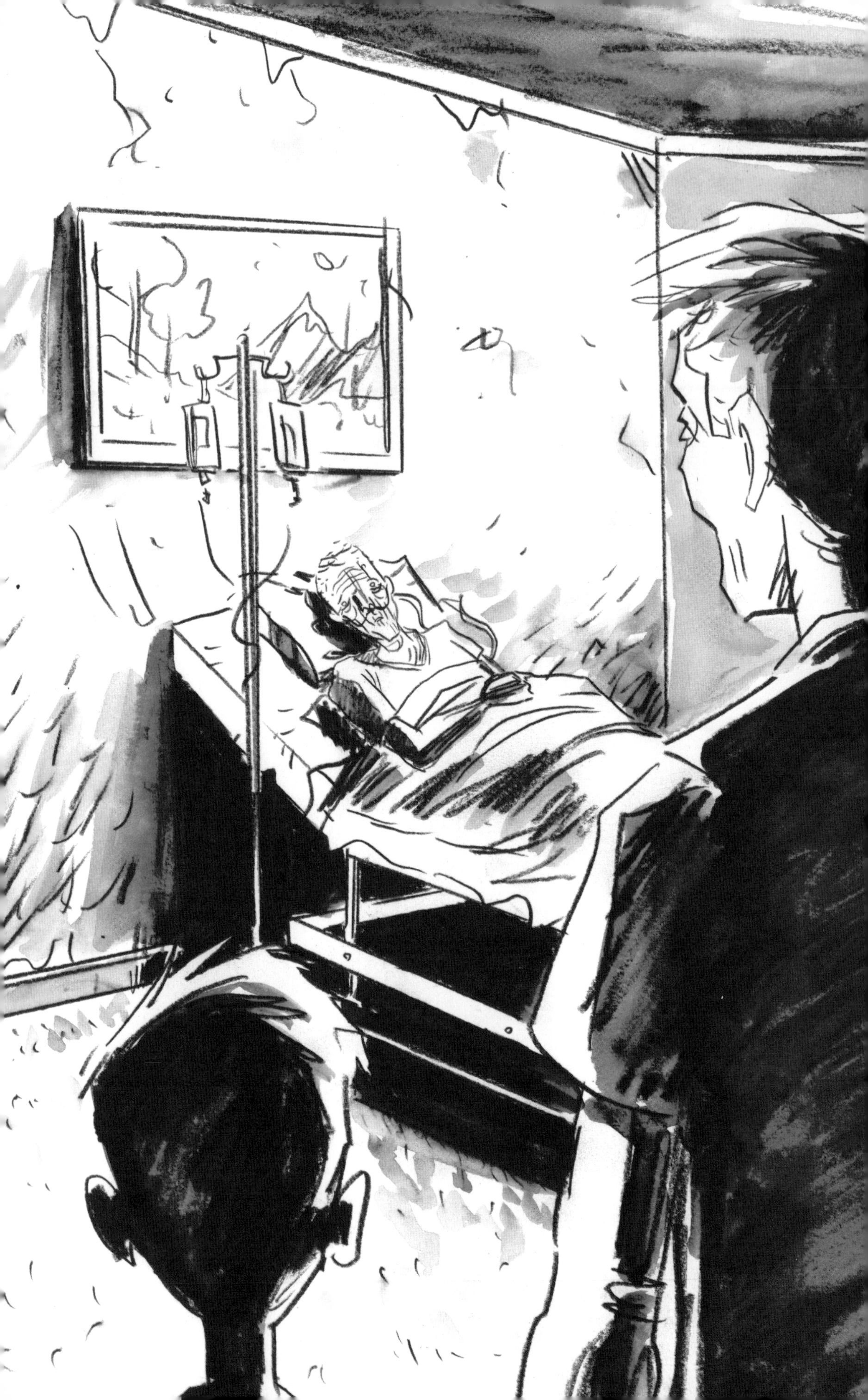

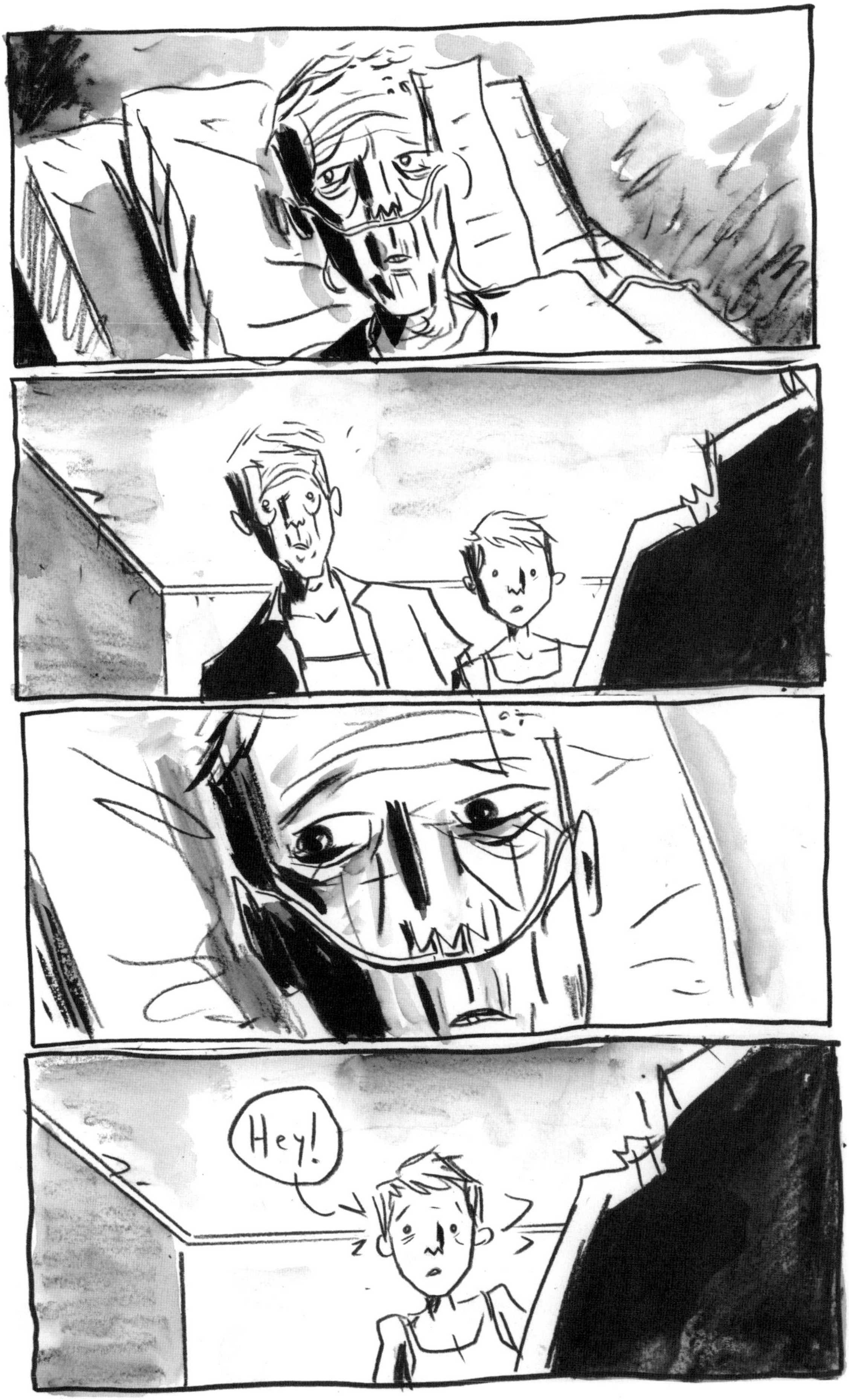
Hey!

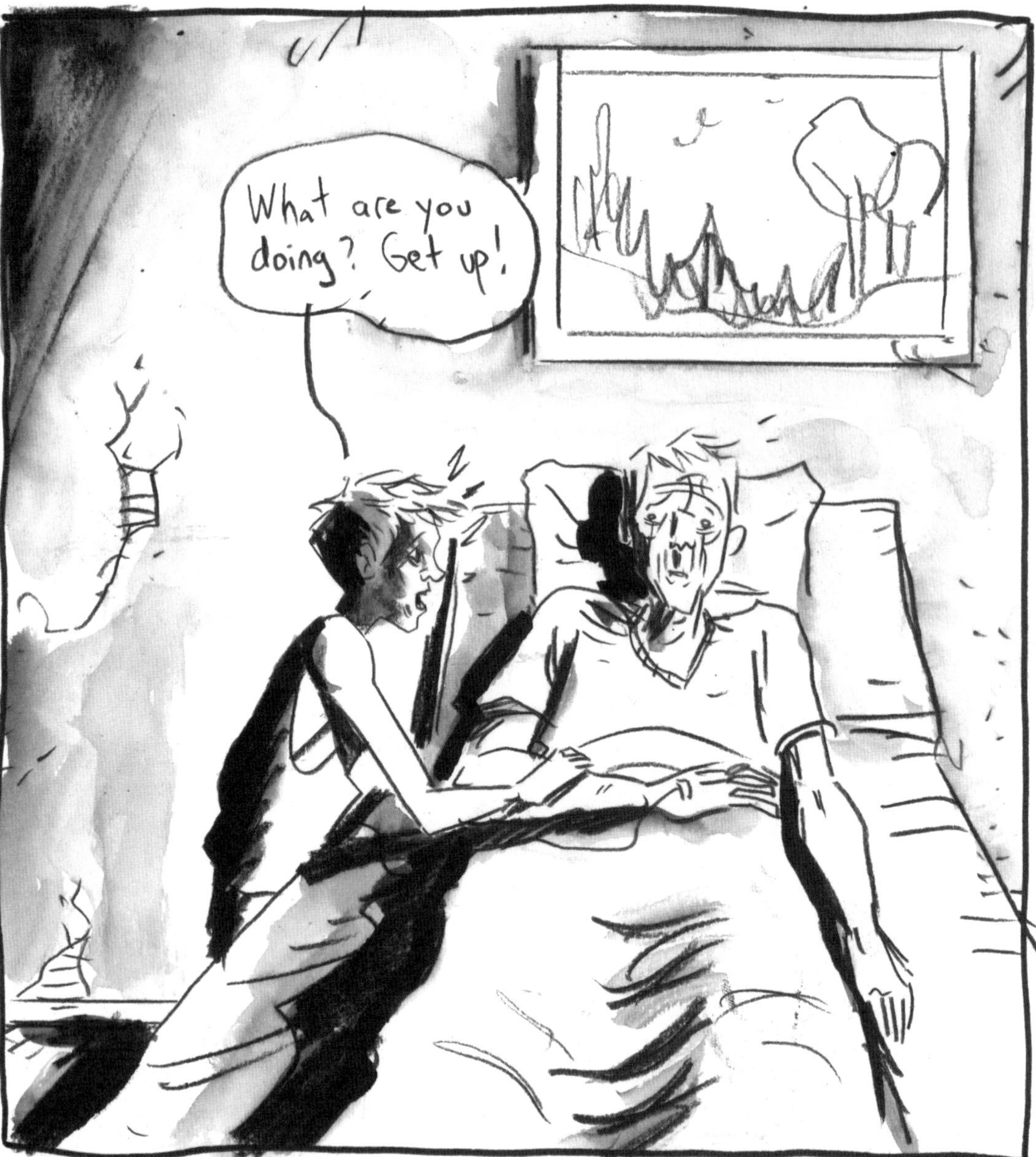
What are you doing? Get up!

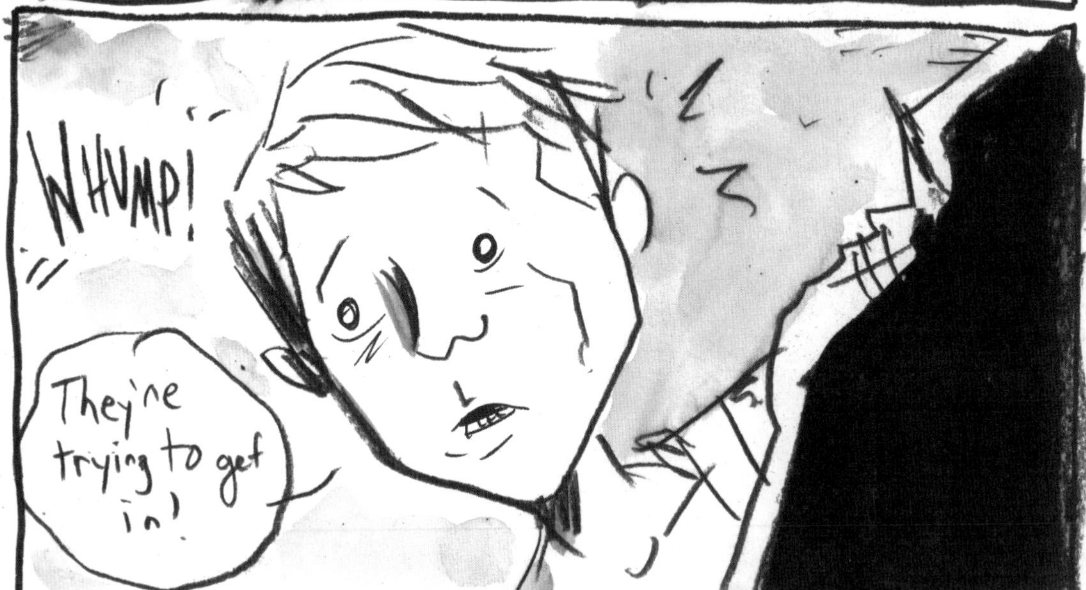
WHUMP!
They're trying to get in!

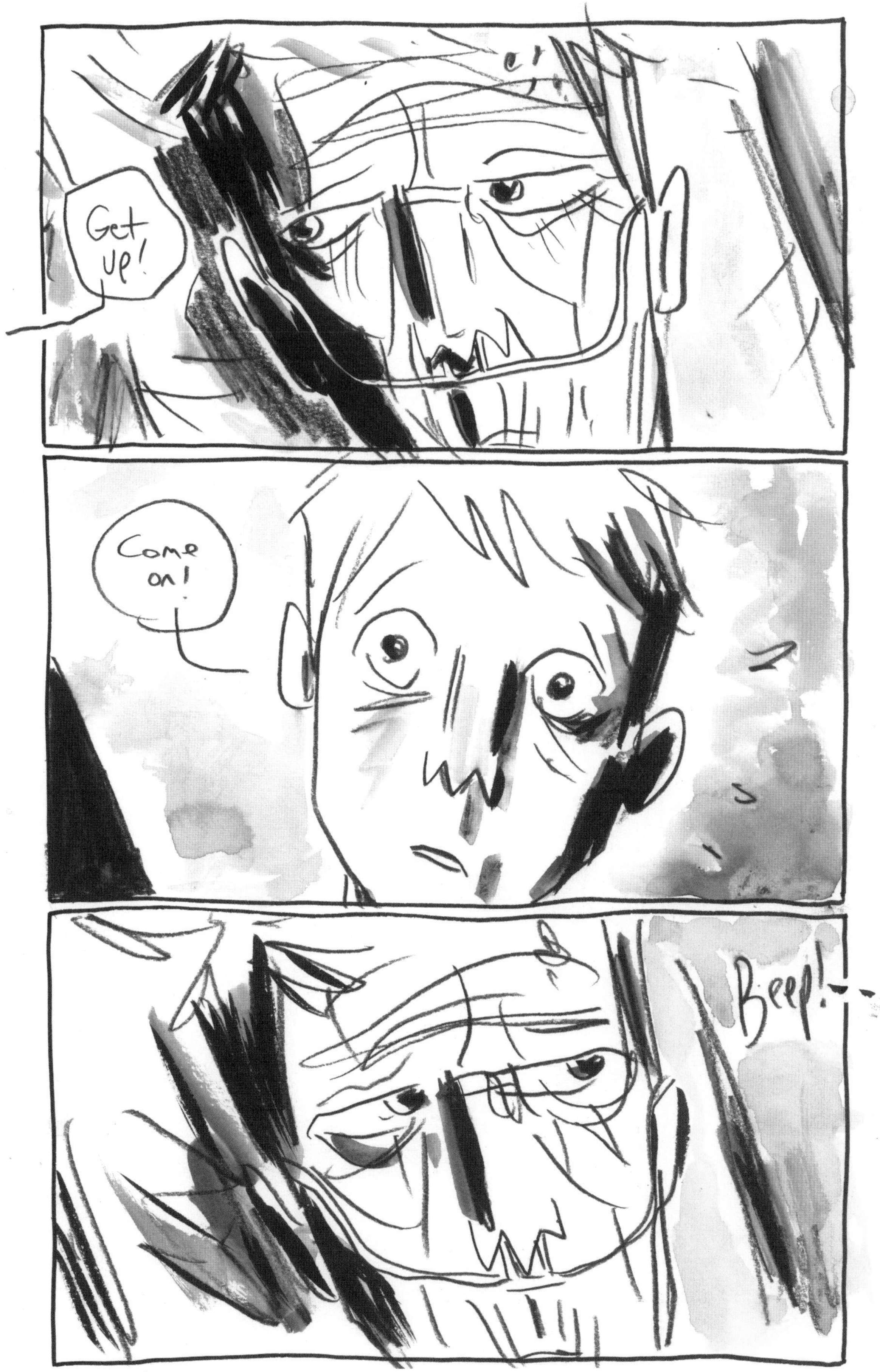
Get up!
Come on!
Beep!

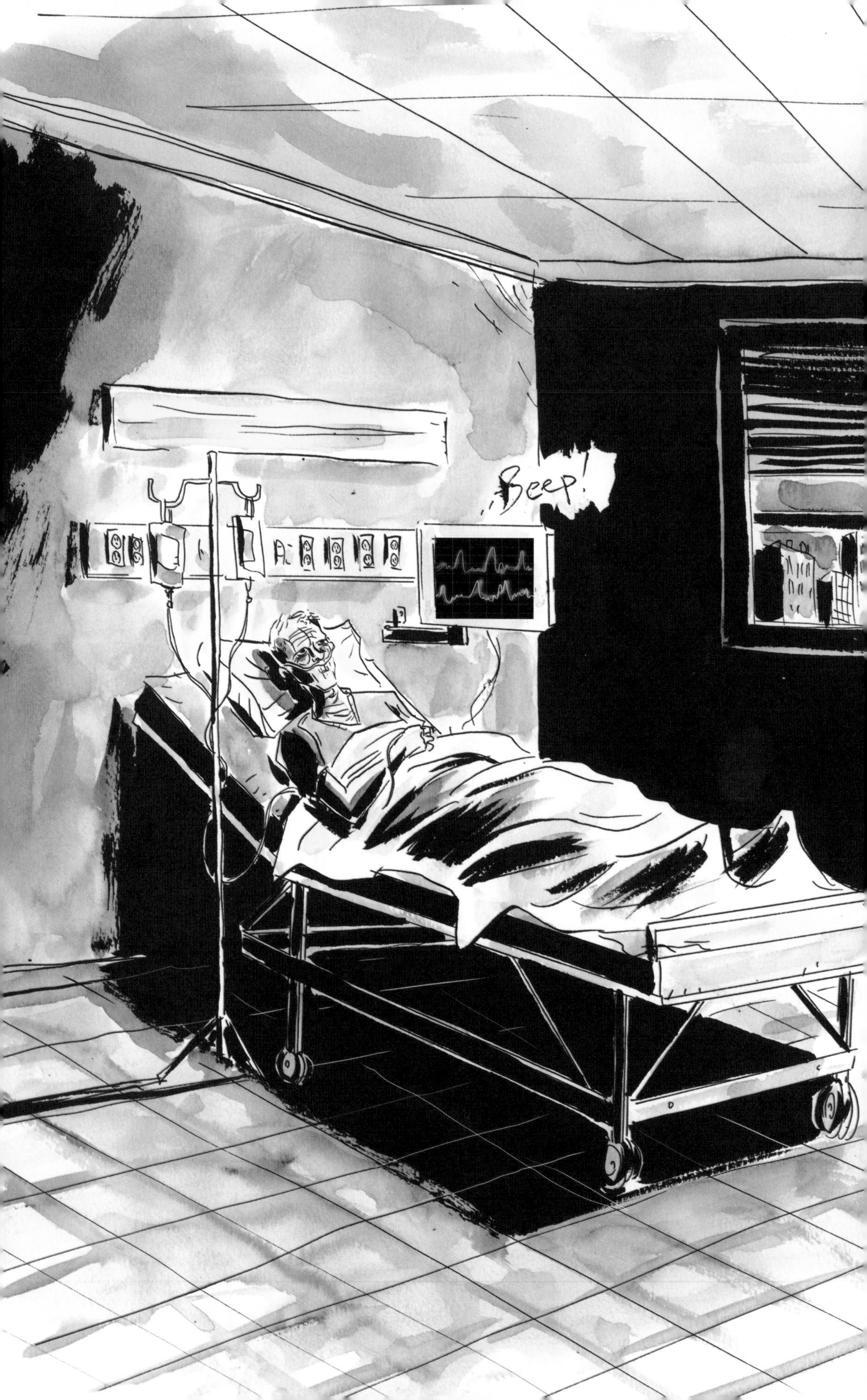
Beep!

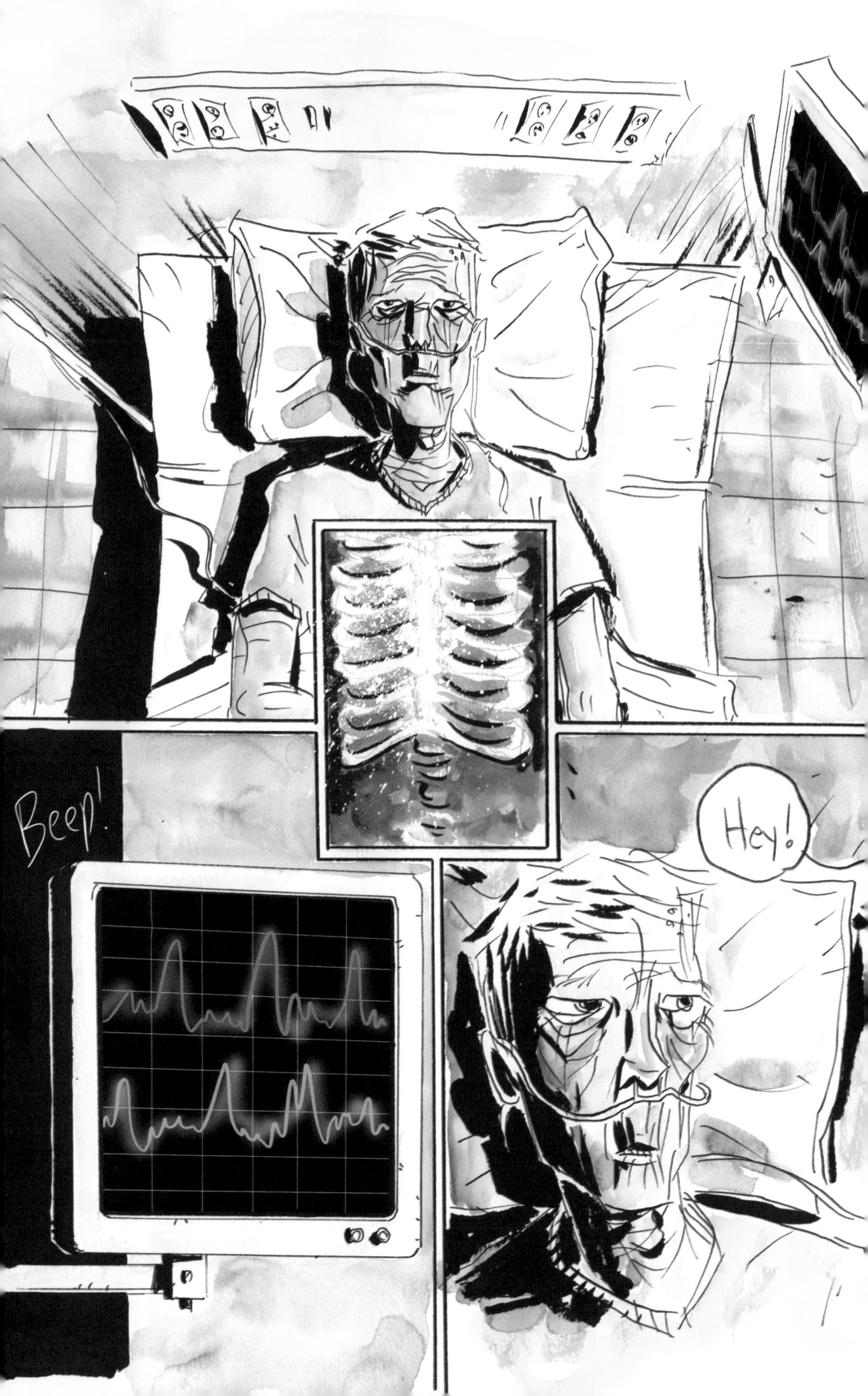
Beep!
Hey!

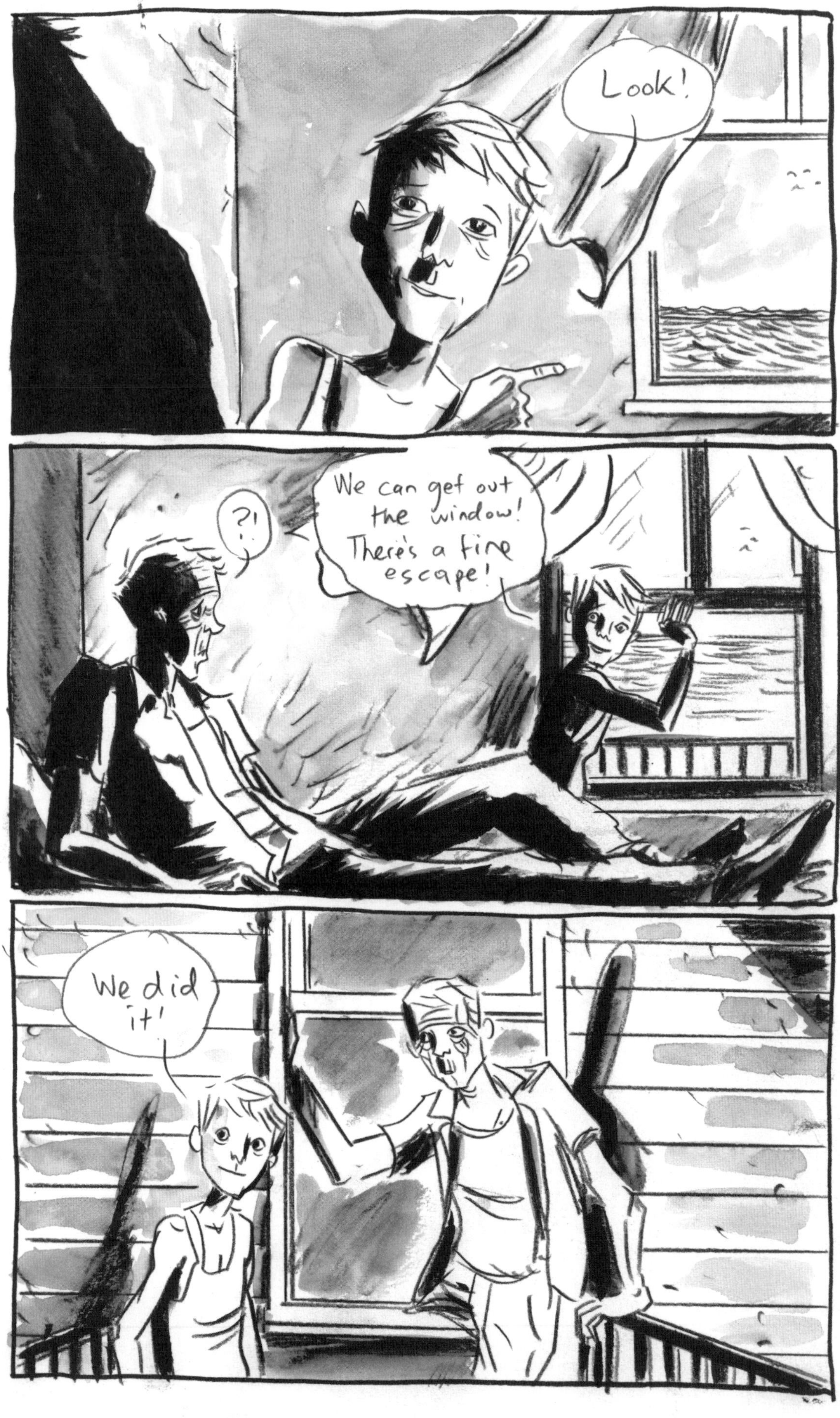
Look!
?!
We can get out the window! There's a fire escape!
We did it!

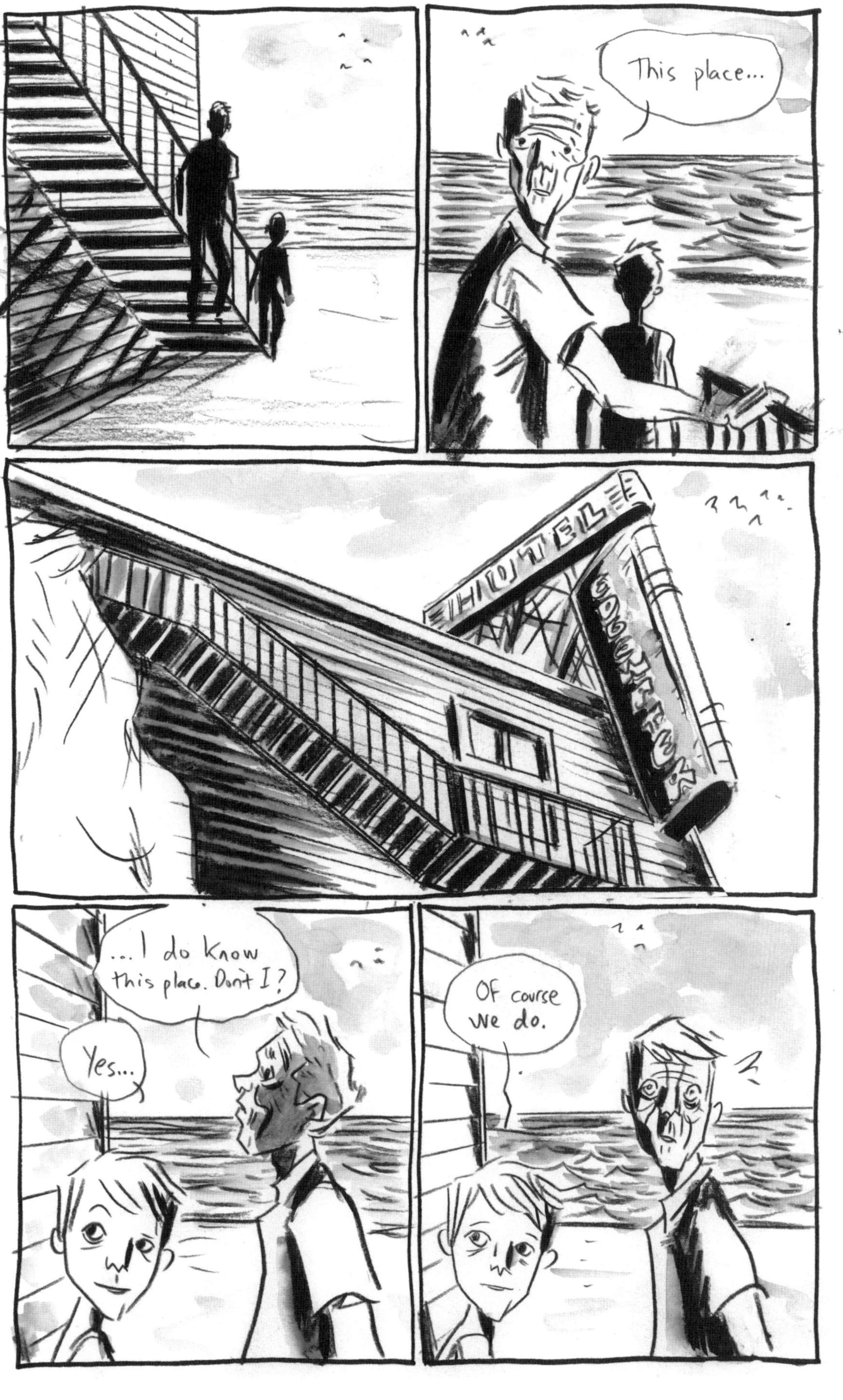
This place...
HOTEL
...I do know this place. Don't I?
Yes...
Of course we do.

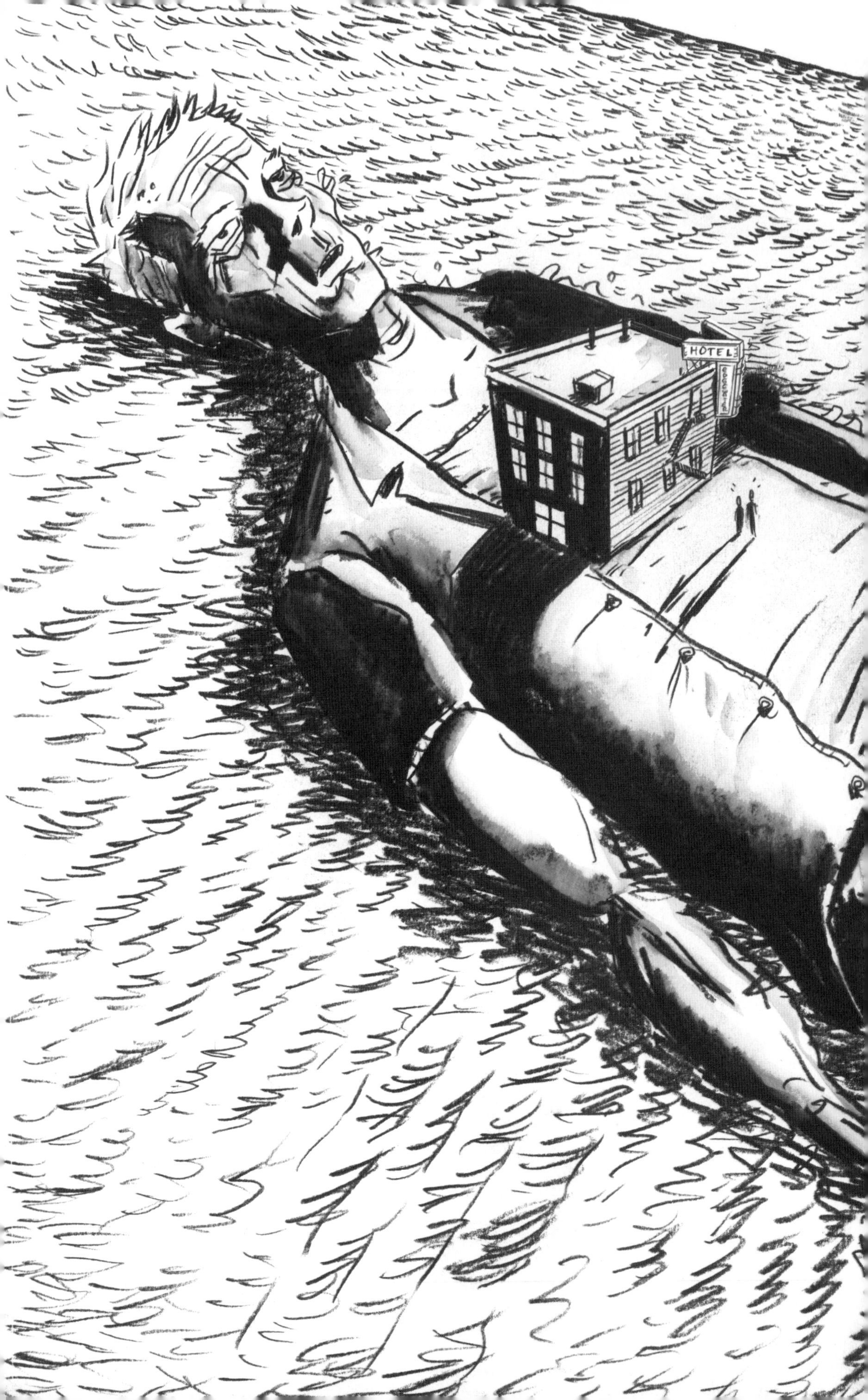
HOTEL

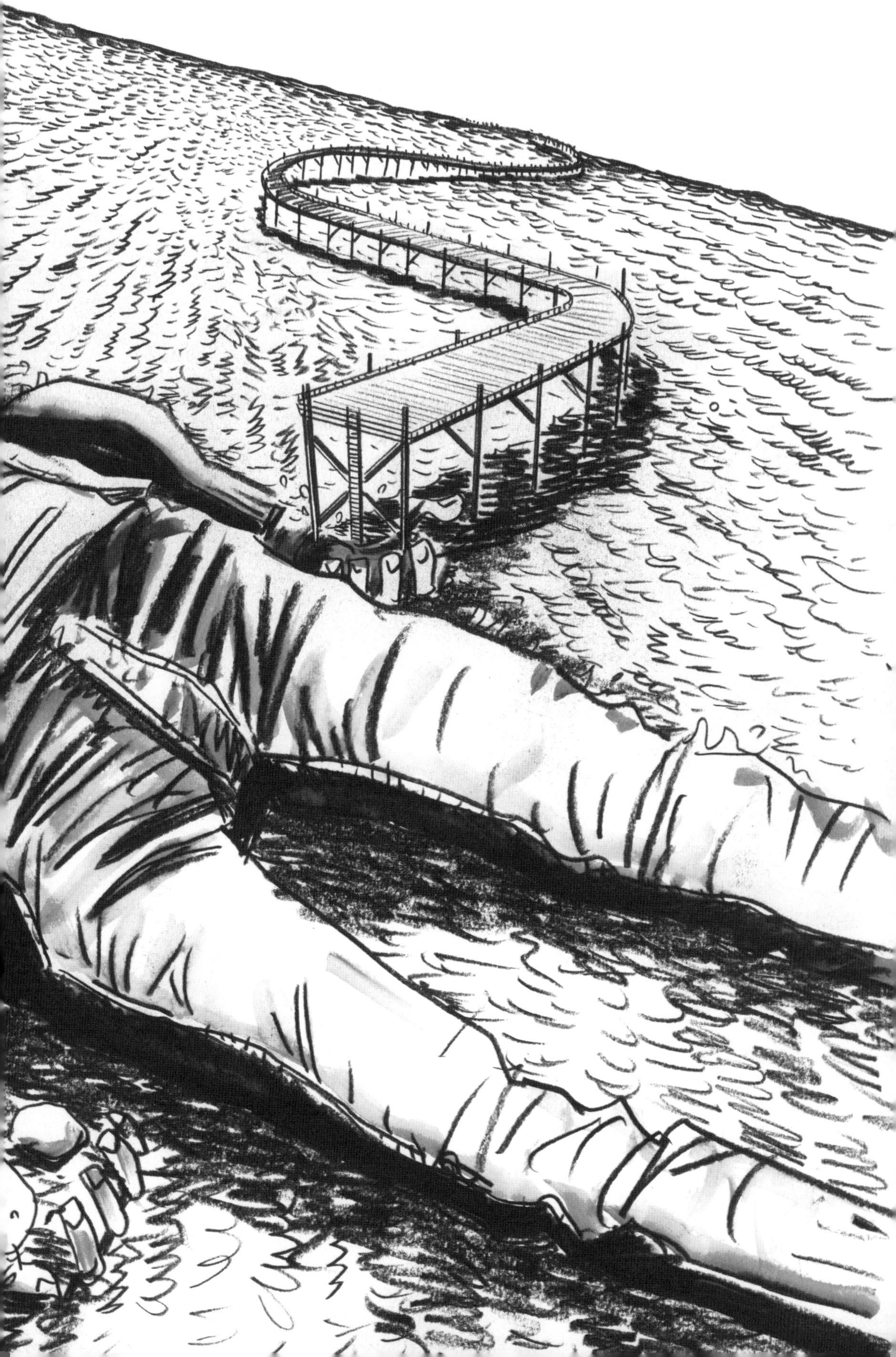

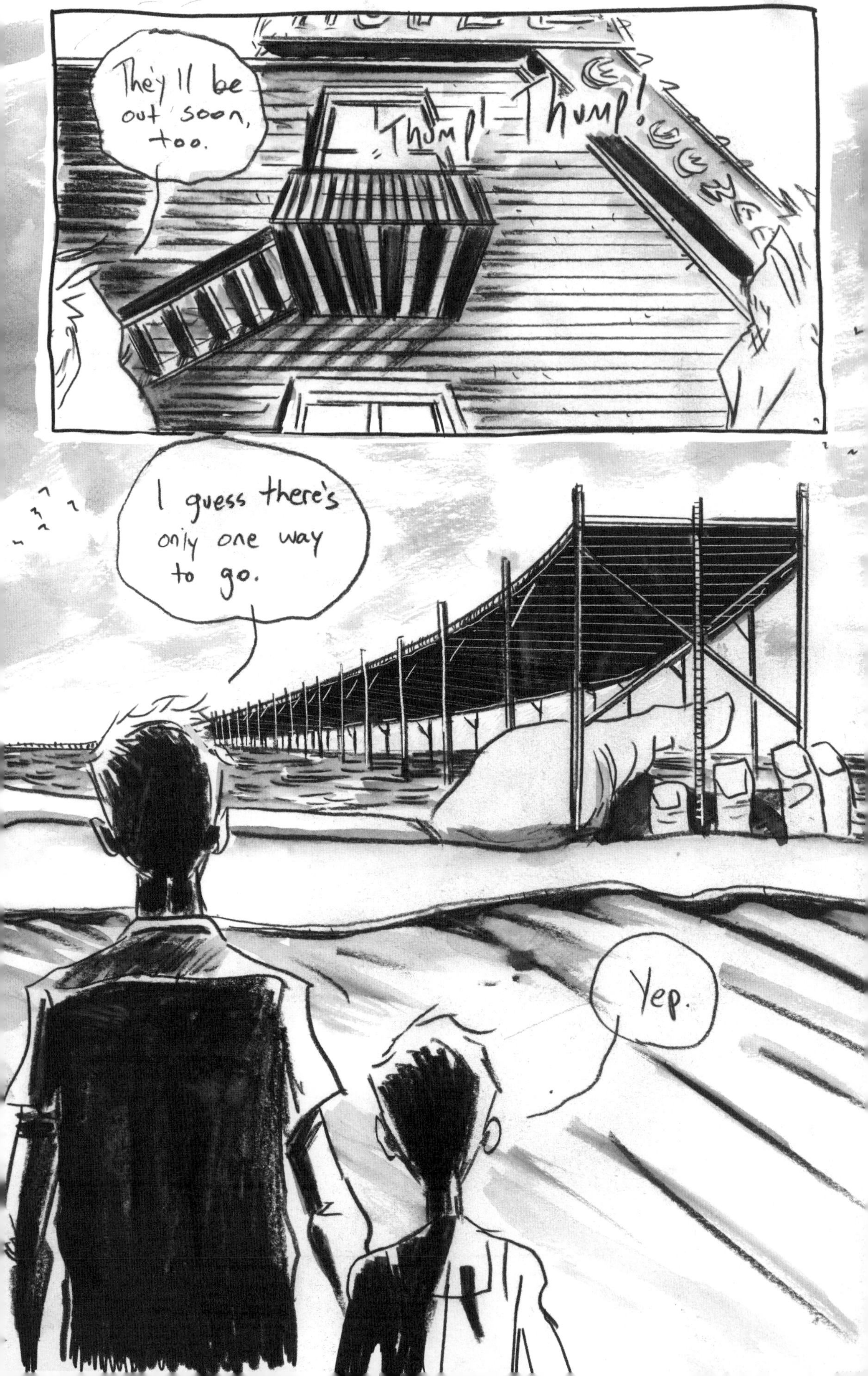
They'll be out soon, too.
THUMP! THUMP!
I guess there's only one way to go.
Yep.

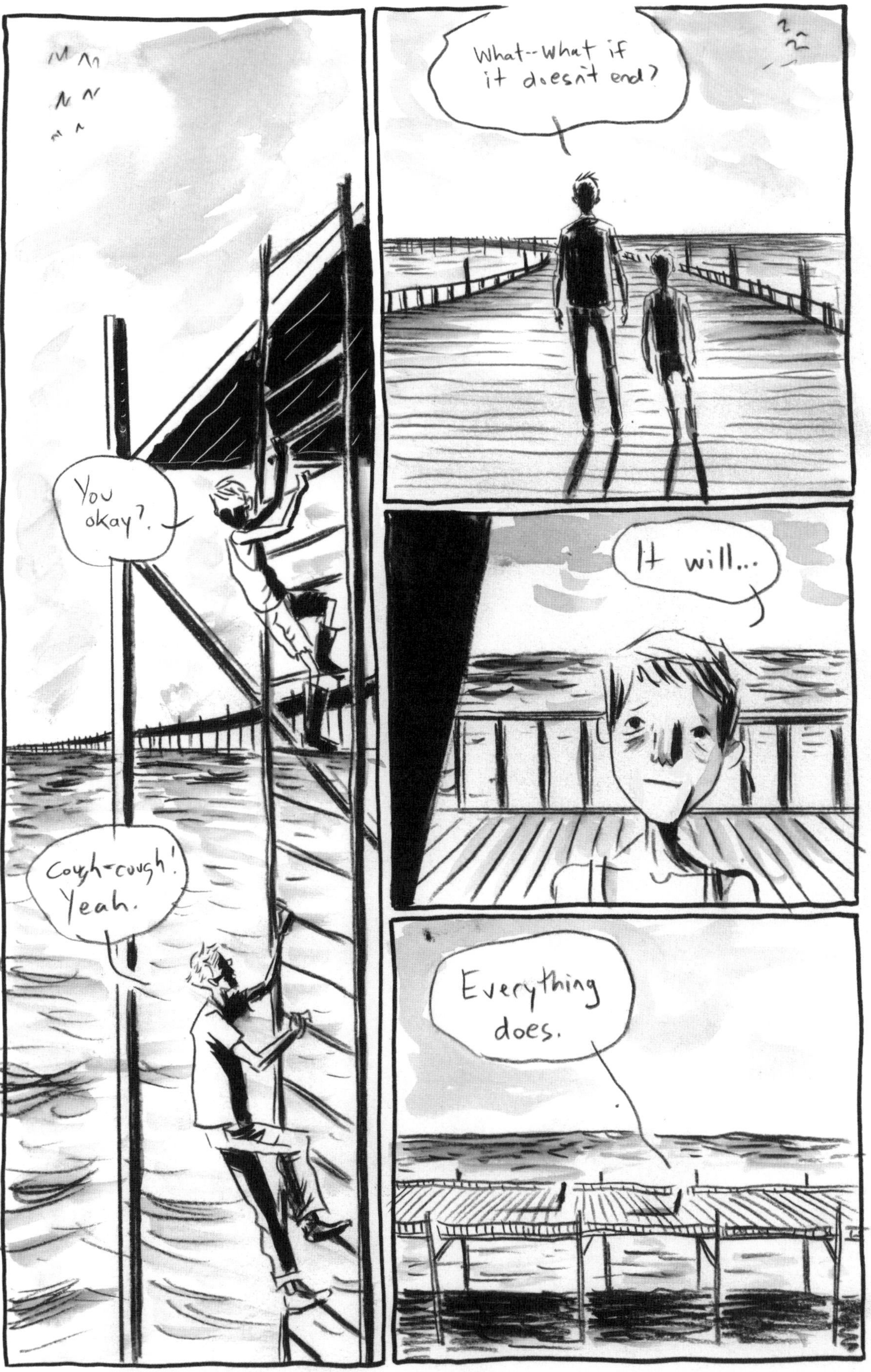
You okay?.
Cough-cough! Yeah.
What--what if it doesn't end?
It will...
Everything does.

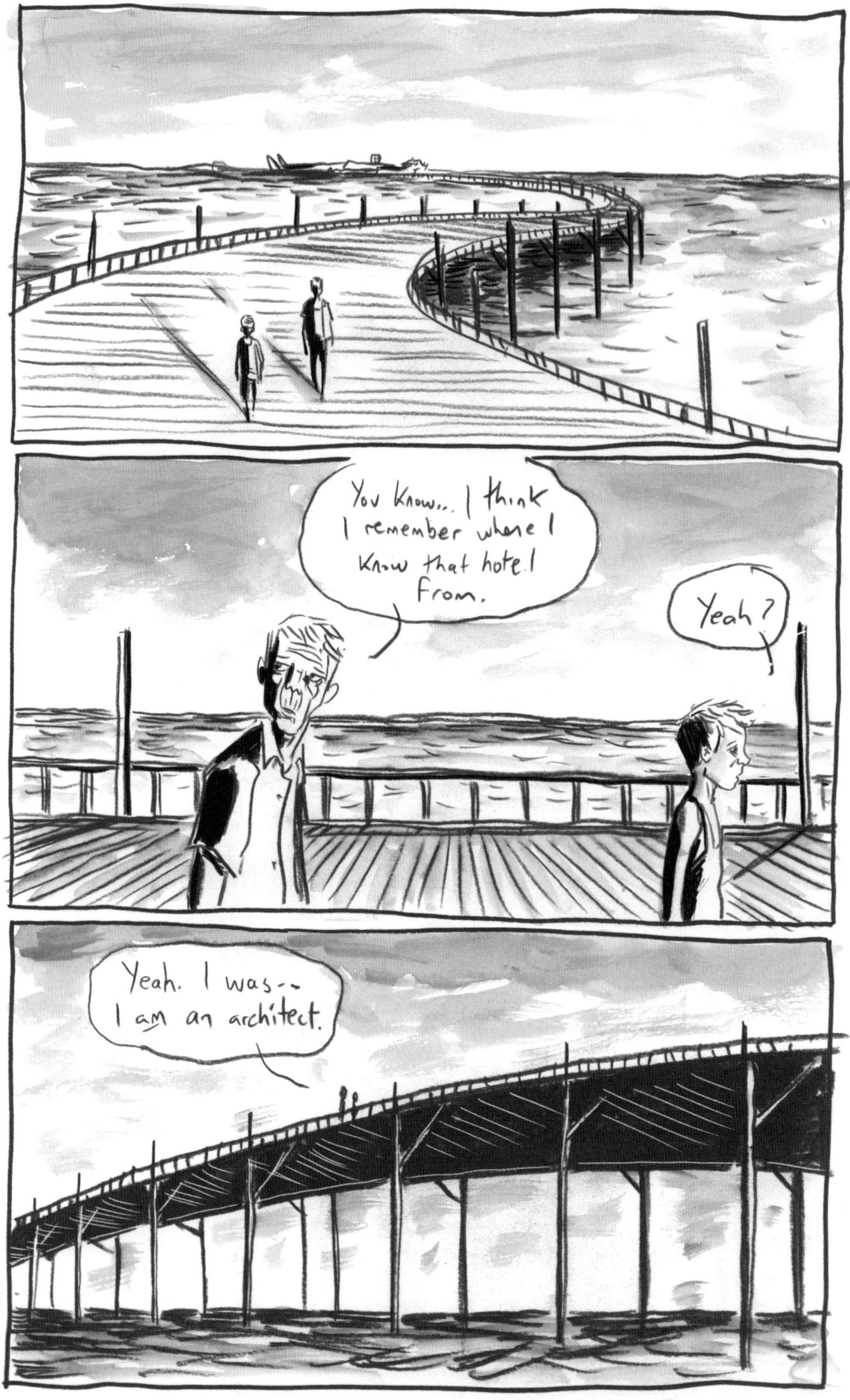
You know... I think I remember where I know that hotel from.
Yeah?
Yeah. I was--
I am an architect.

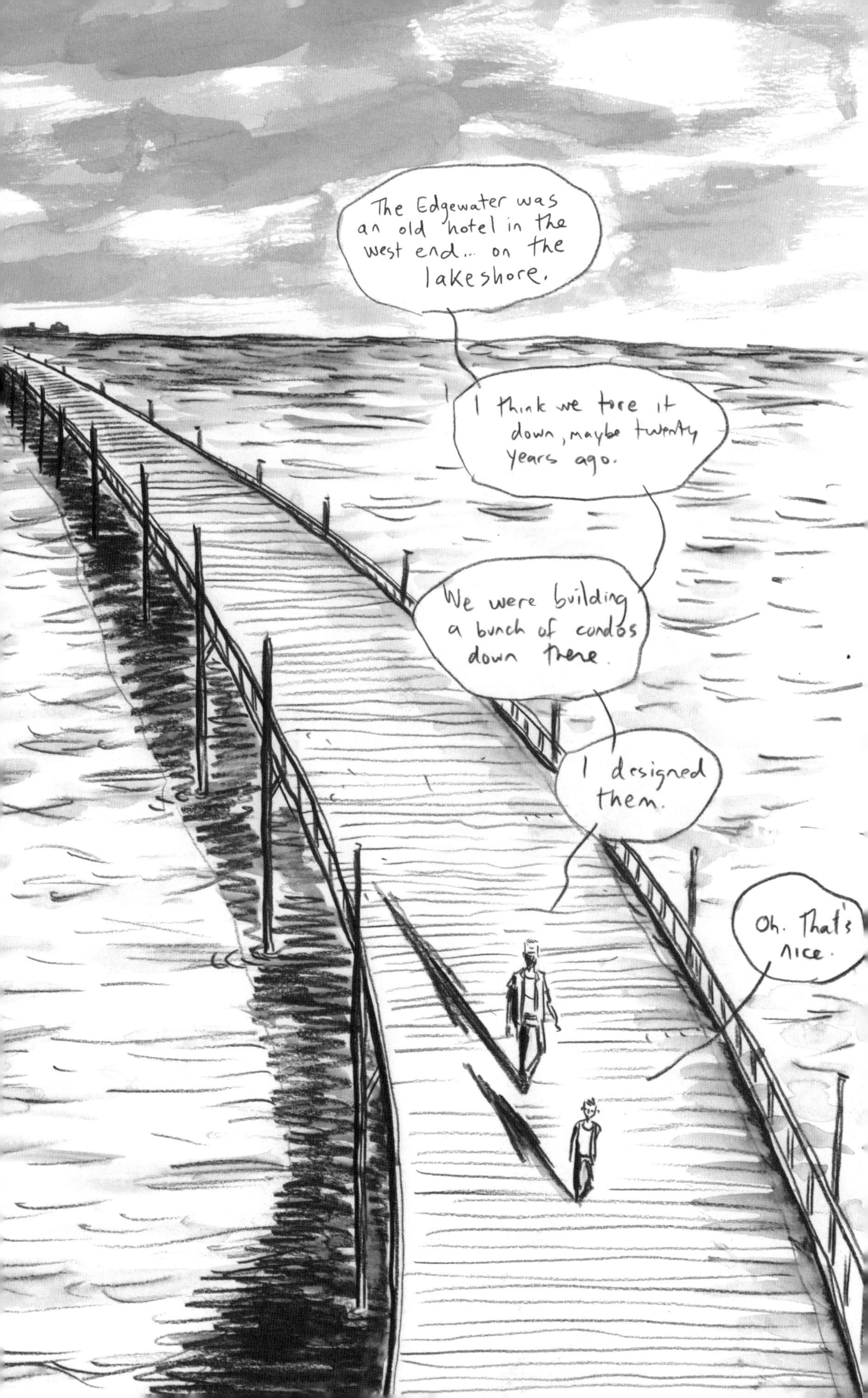
The Edgewater was an old hotel in the west end... on the lakeshore.
I think we tore it down, maybe twenty years ago.
We were building a bunch of condos down there.
I designed them.
Oh. That's nice.

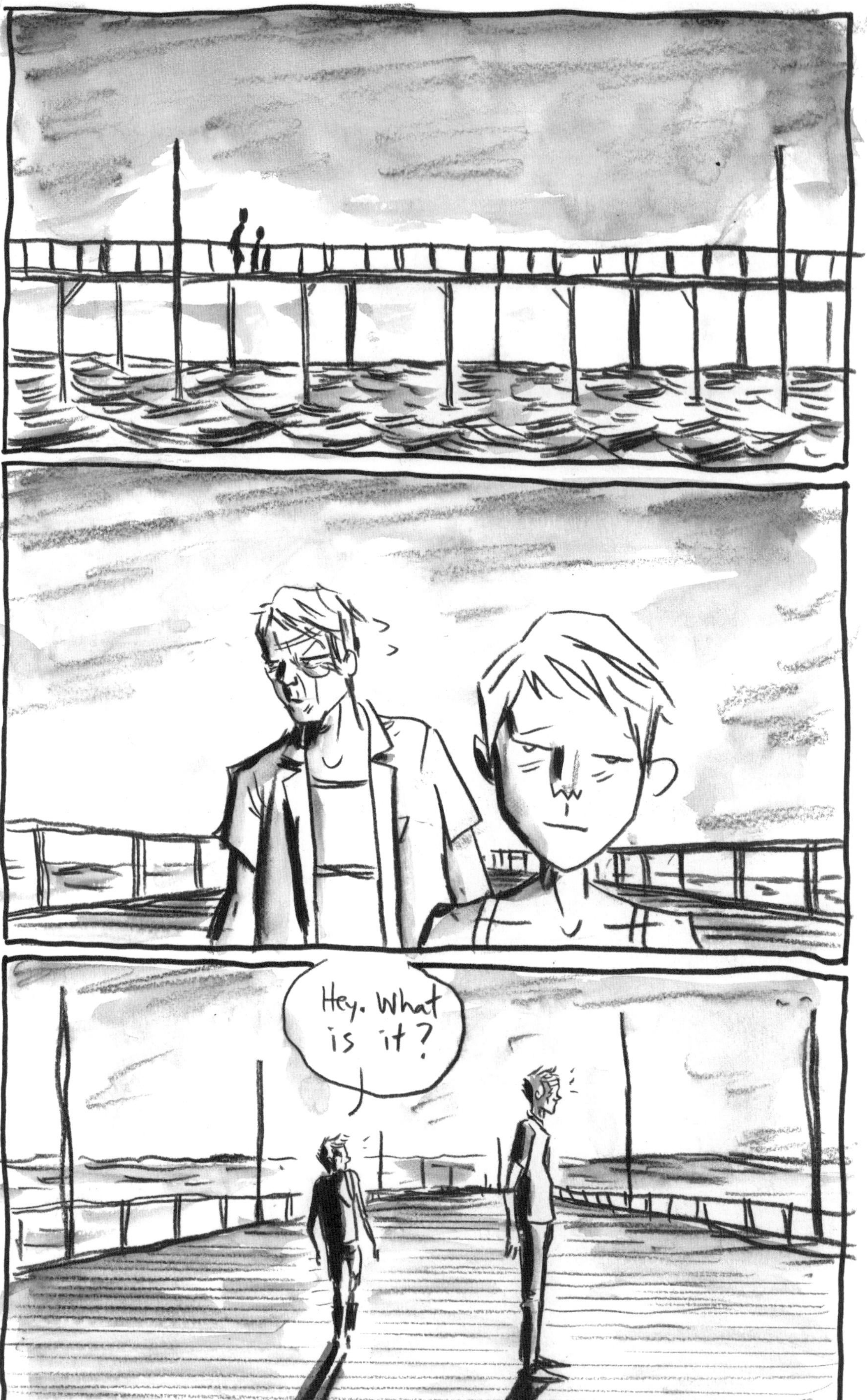
Hey. What is it?

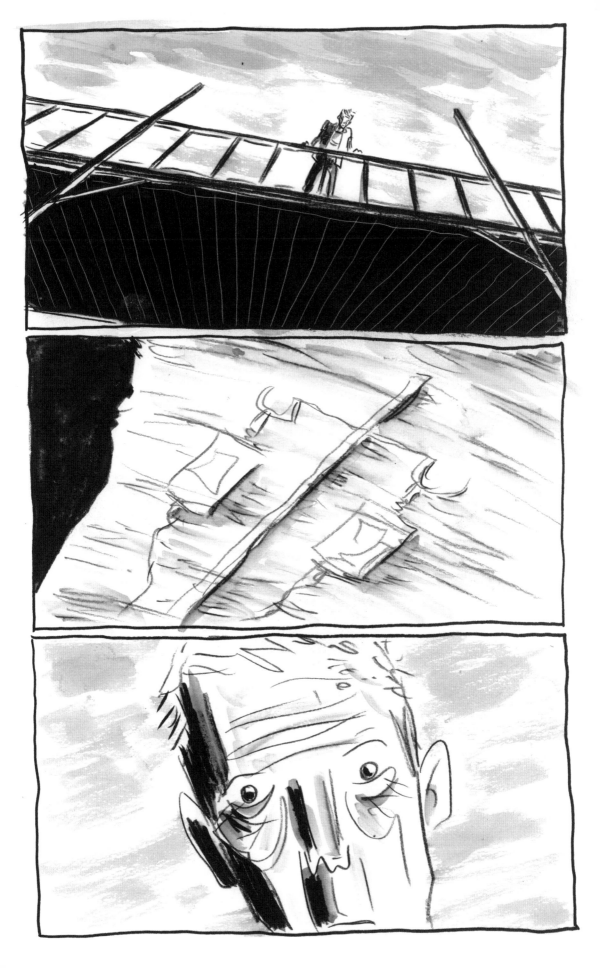

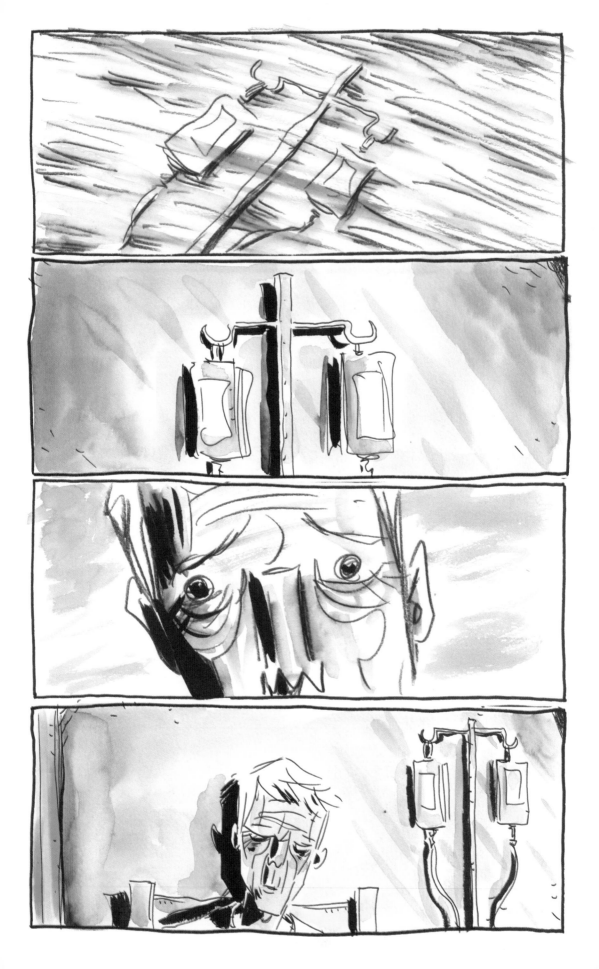

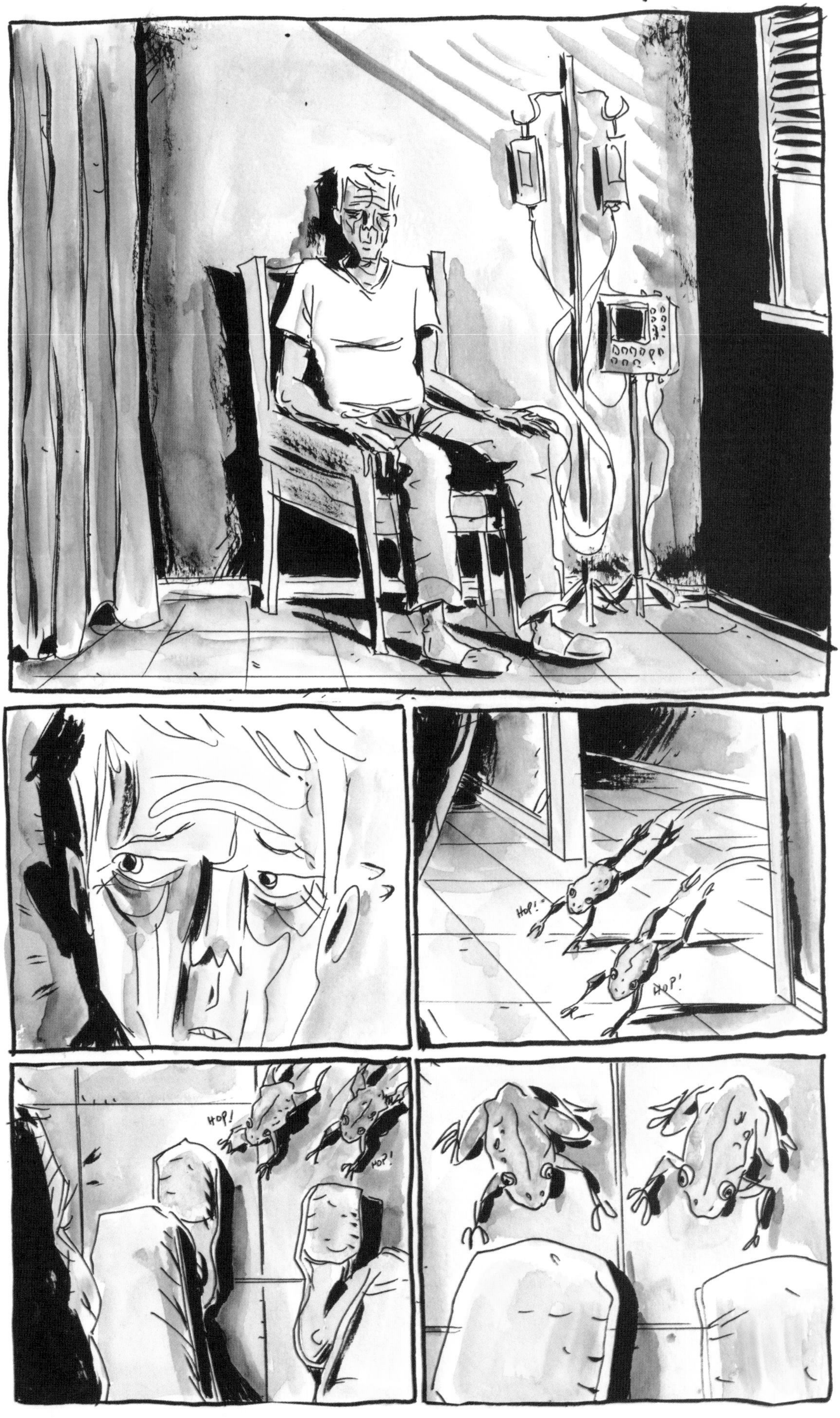
HOP!
HOP!
HOP!
HOP!

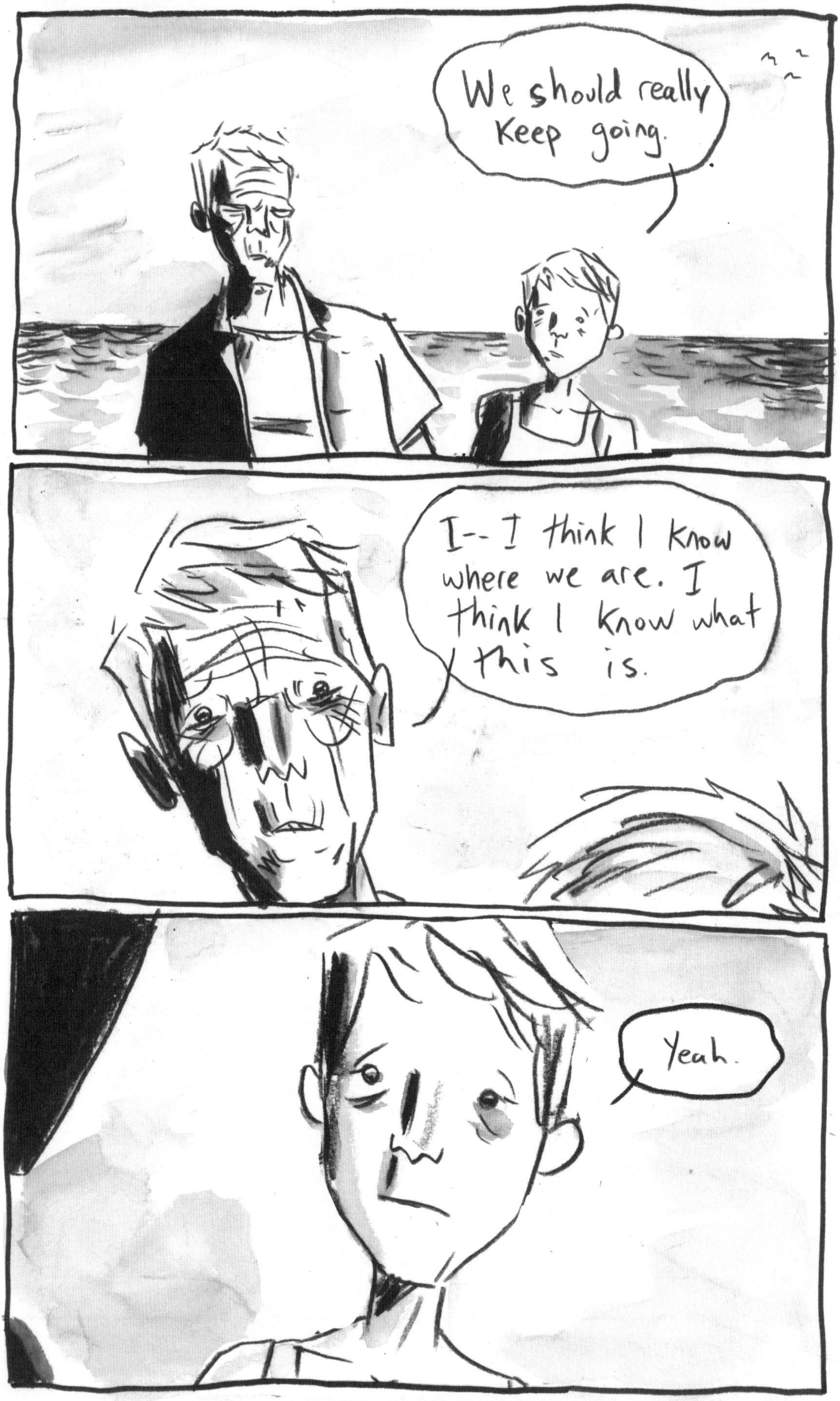
We should really keep going.
I-- I think I know where we are. I think I know what this is.
Yeah.

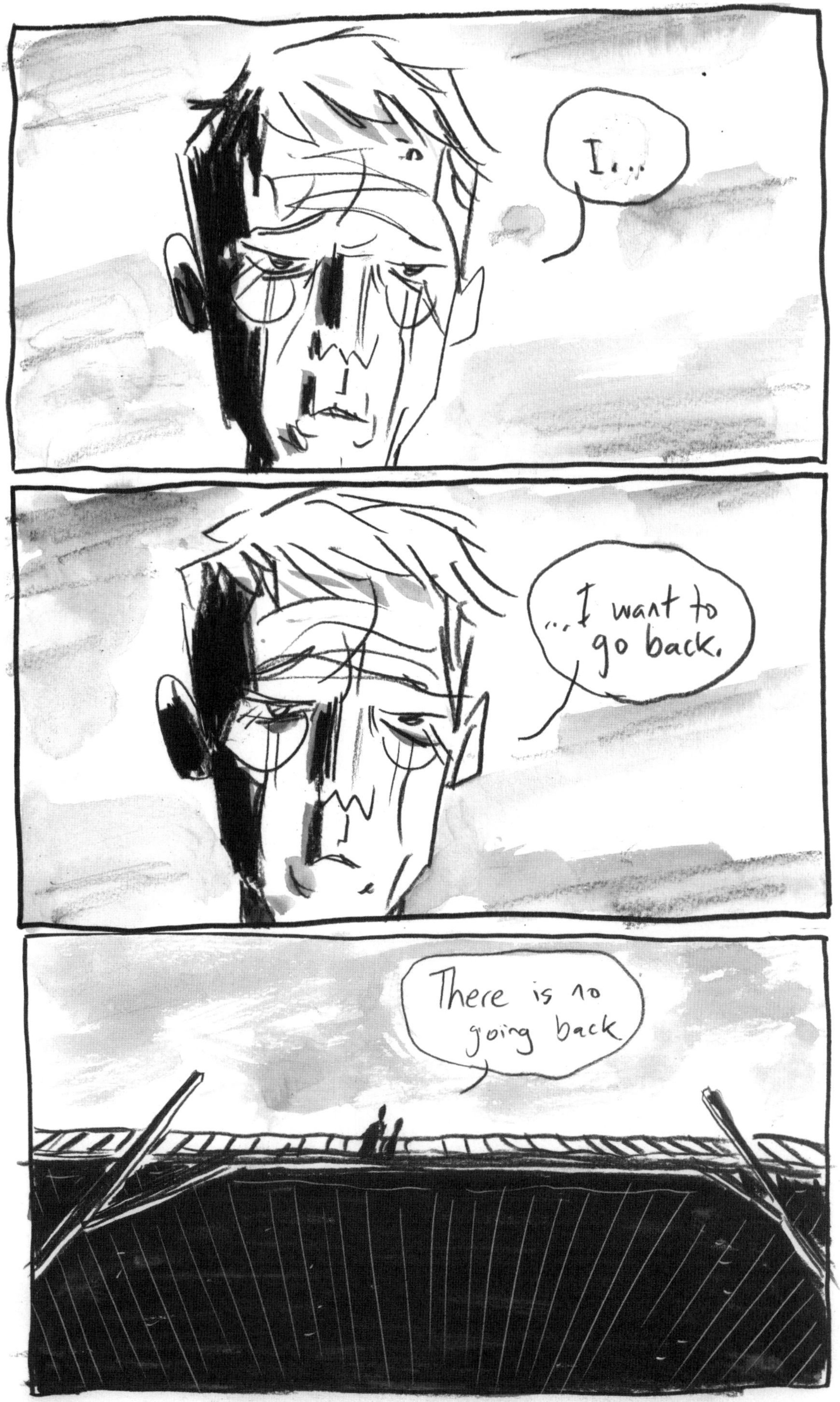
I...
...I want to go back.
There is no going back

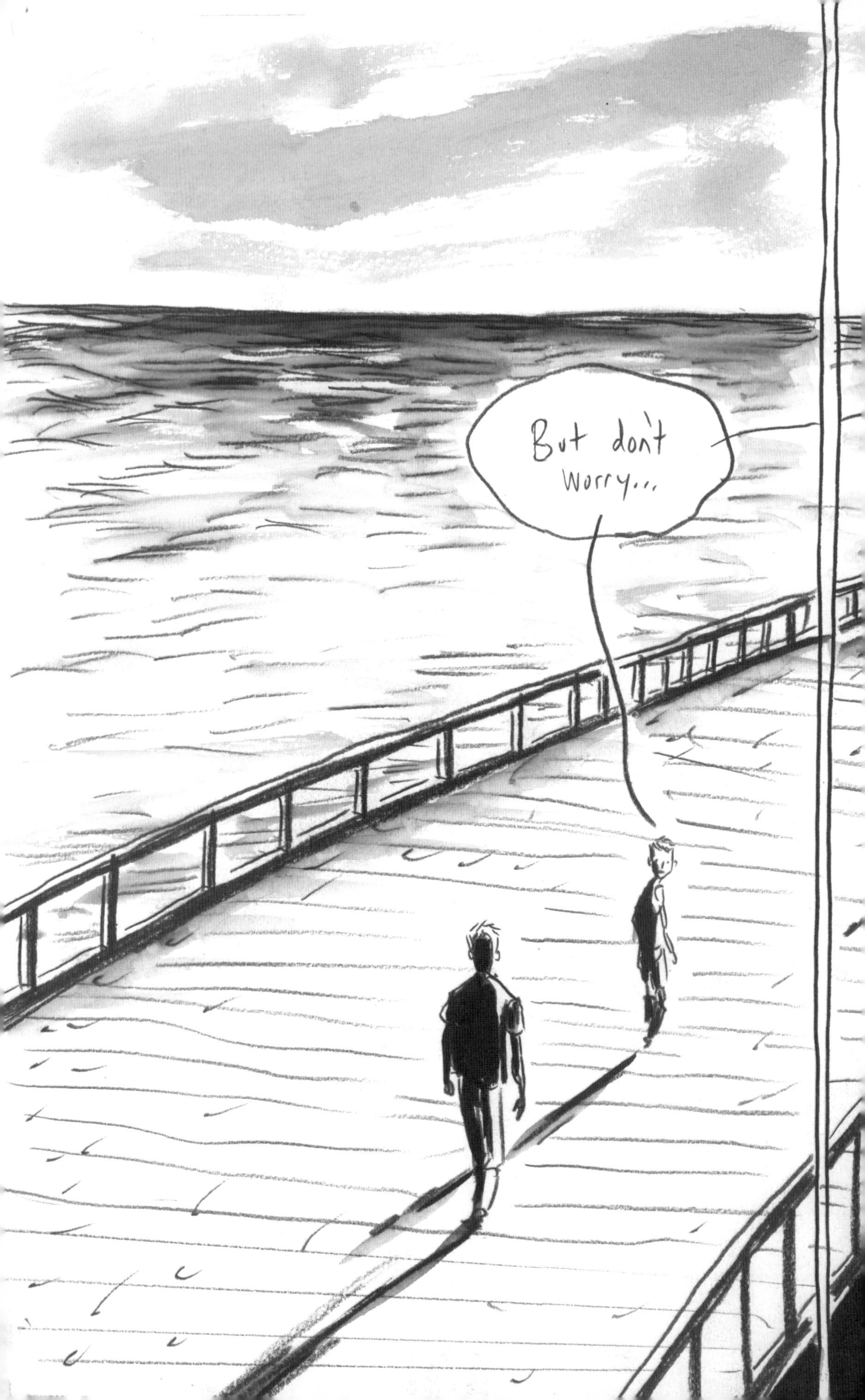
But don't worry...

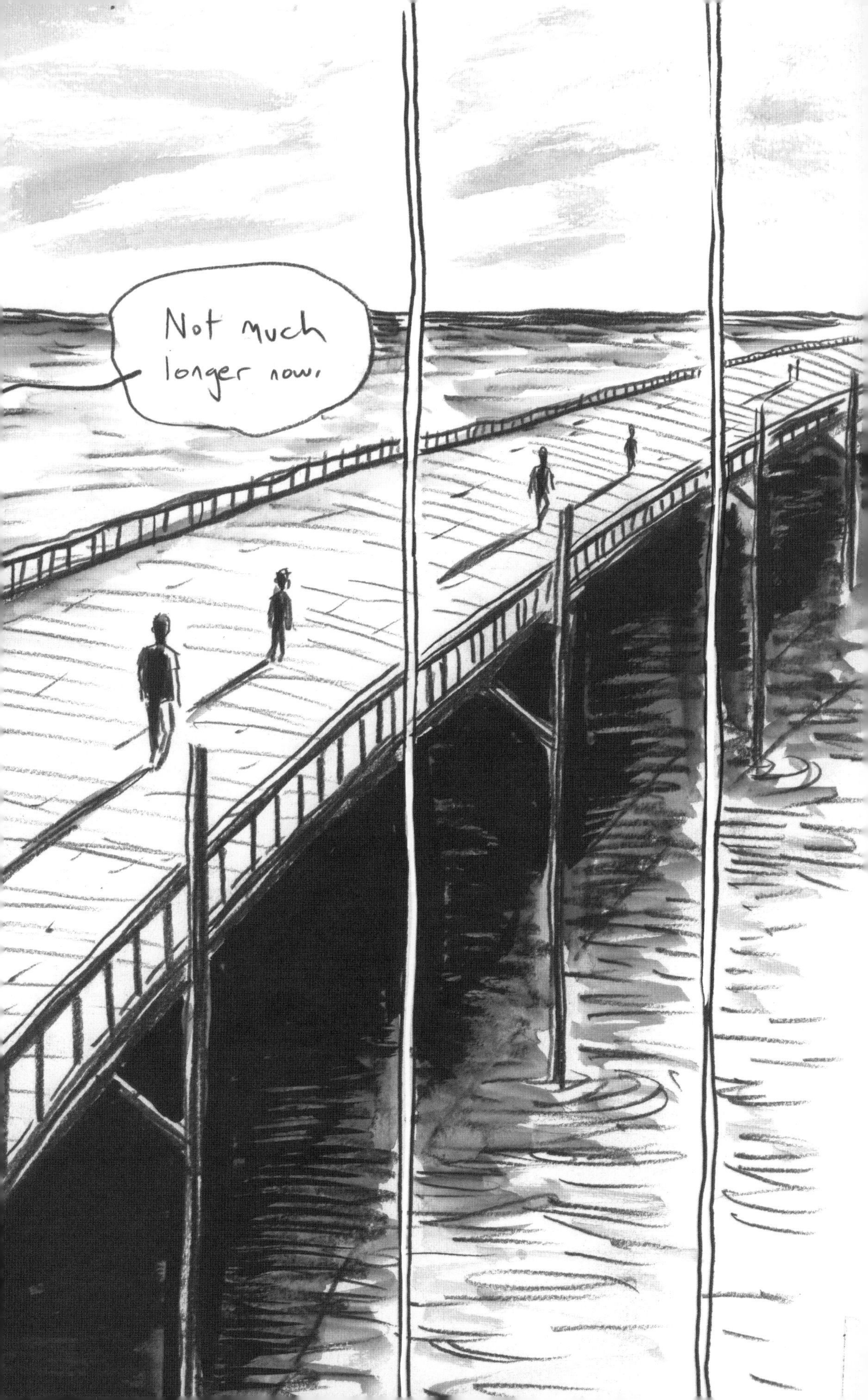
Not much longer now.

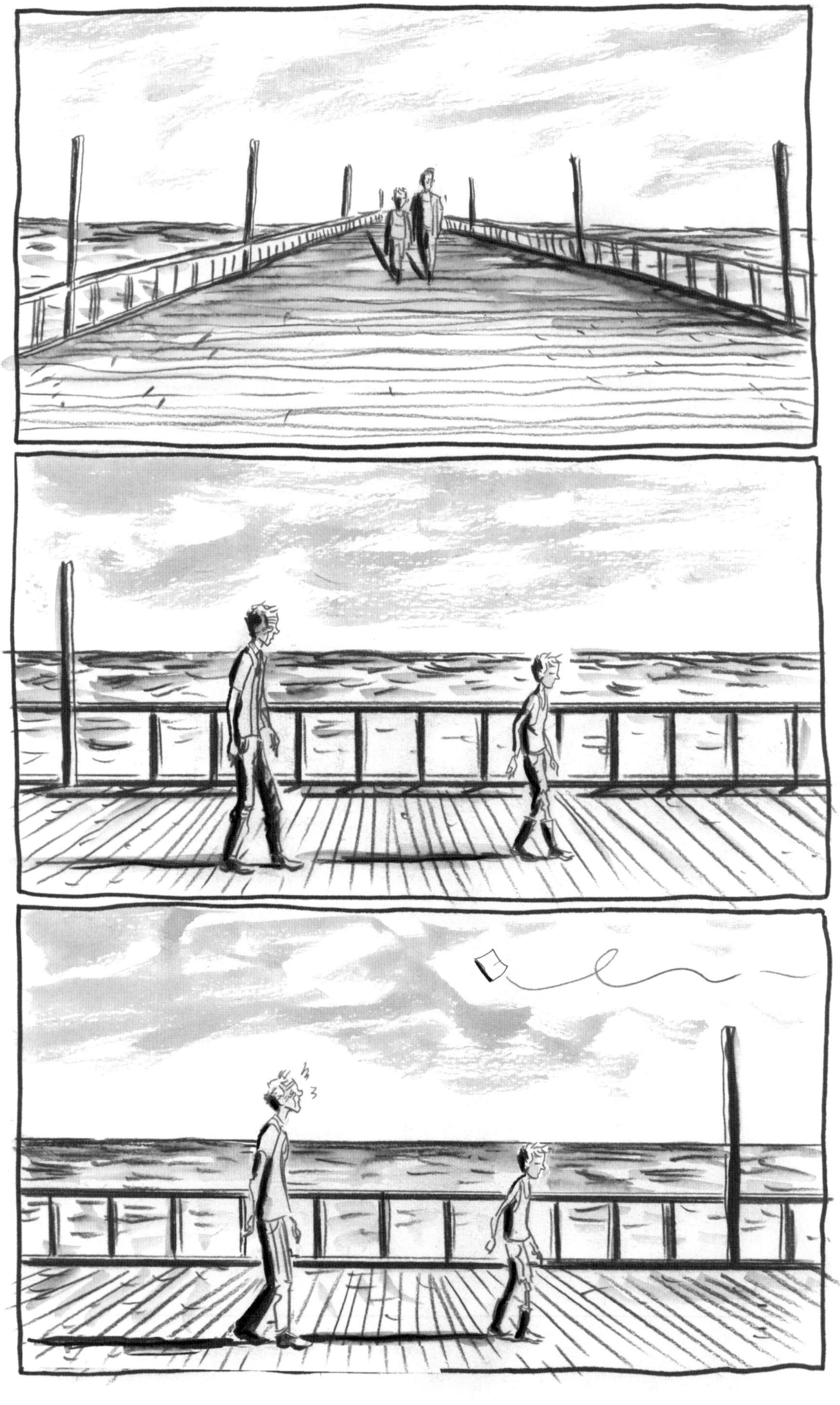

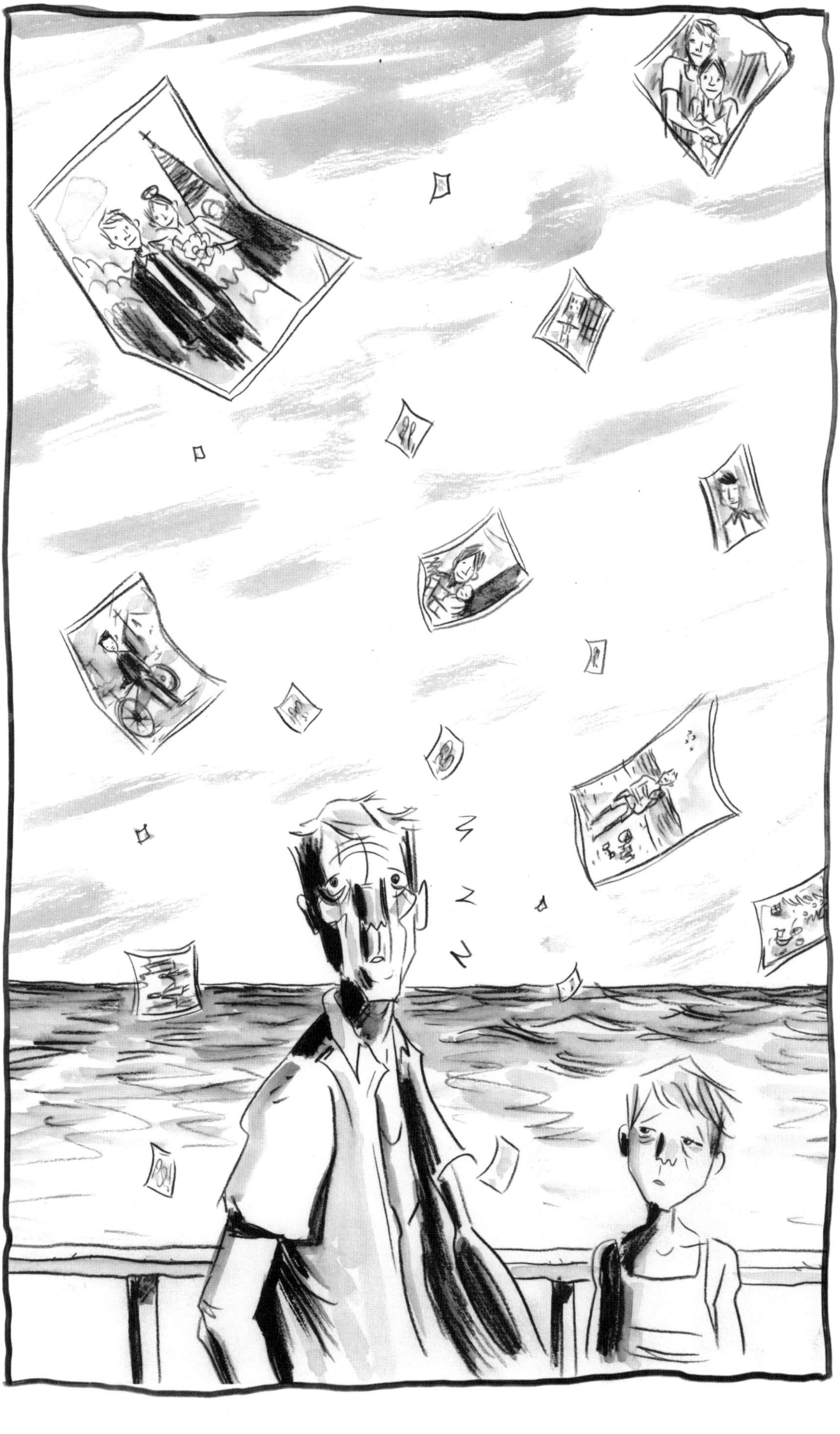

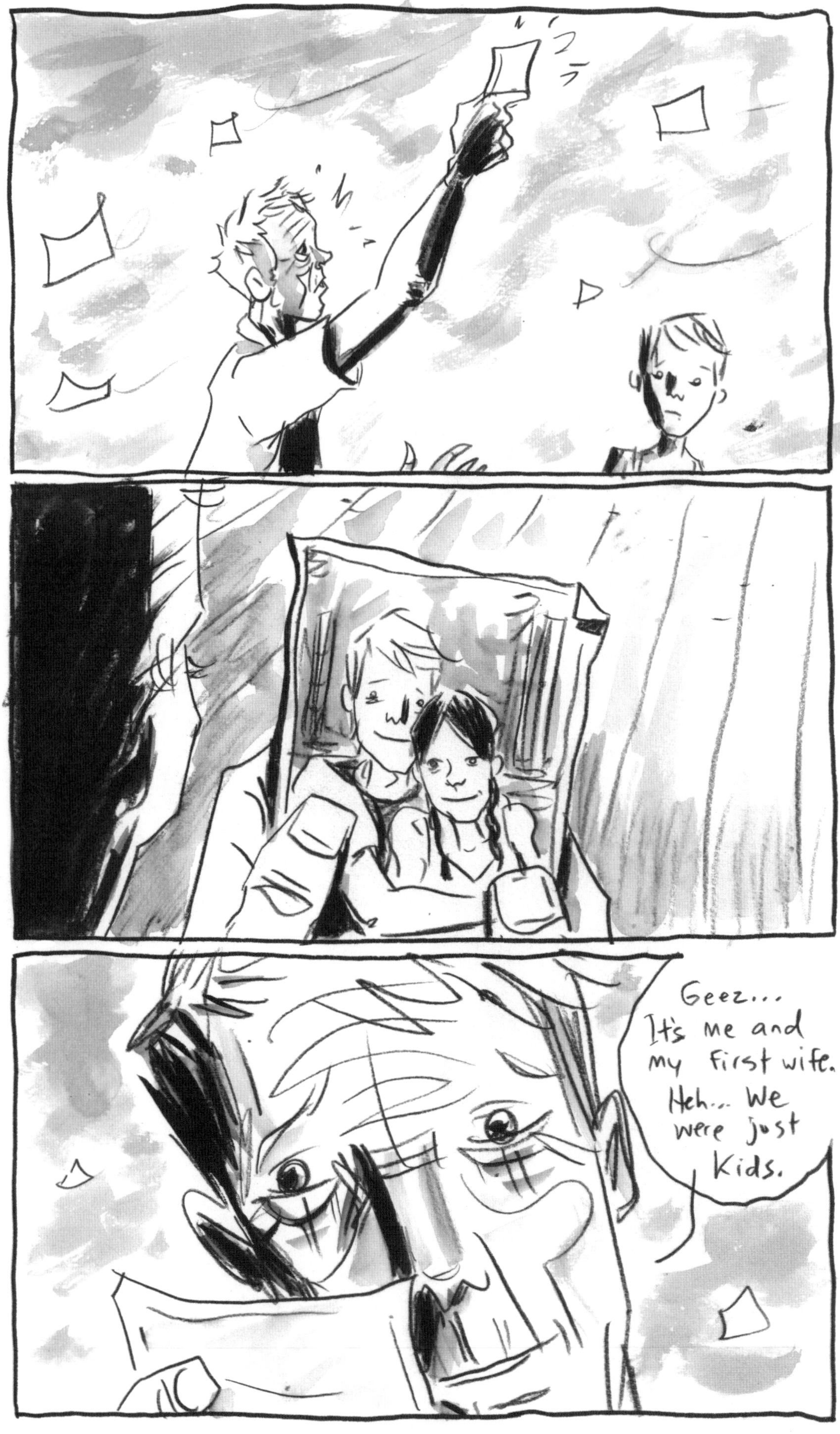
Geez... It's me and my first wife. Heh... We were just kids.

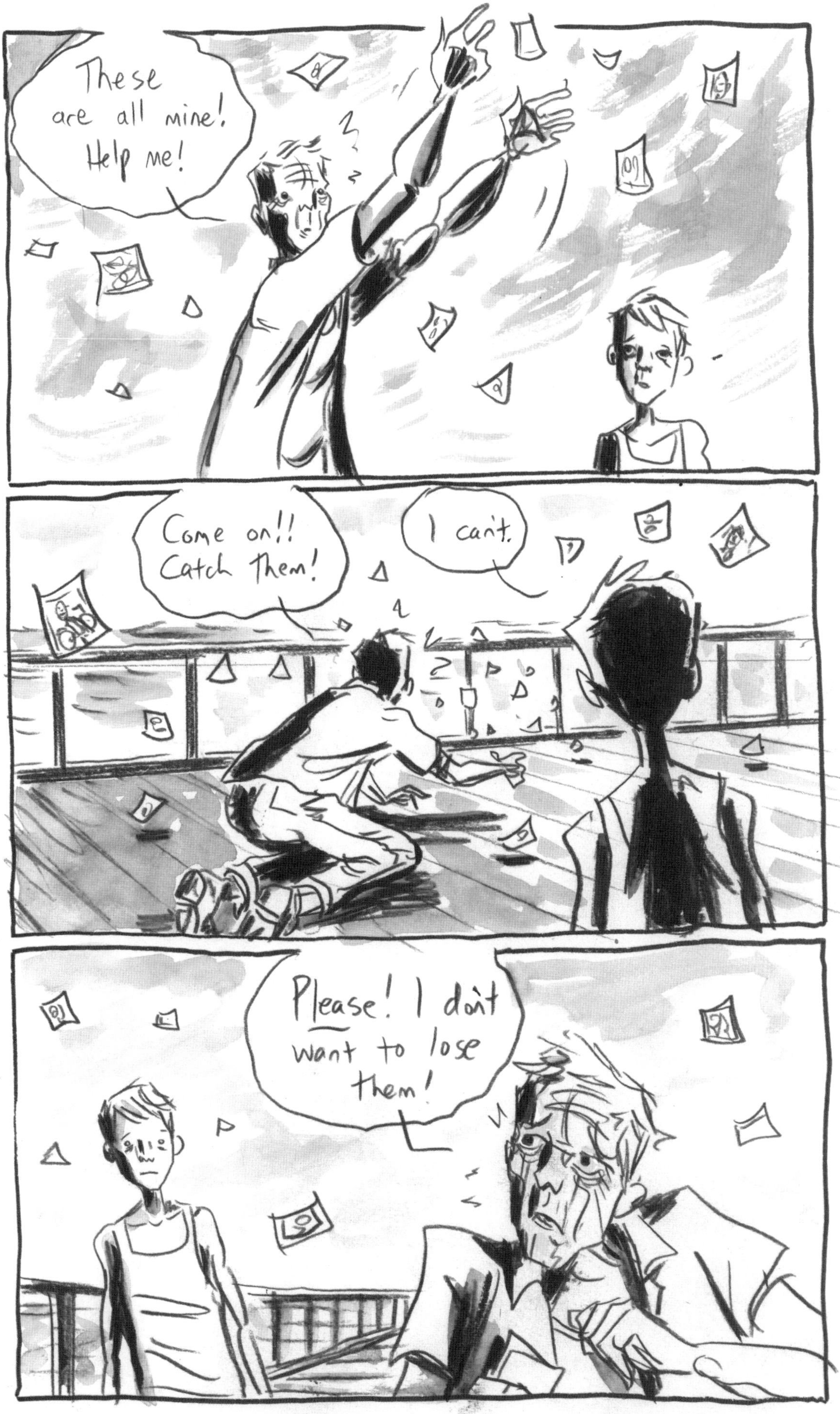
These are all mine! Help me!
Come on!! Catch them!
I can't.
Please! I don't want to lose them!

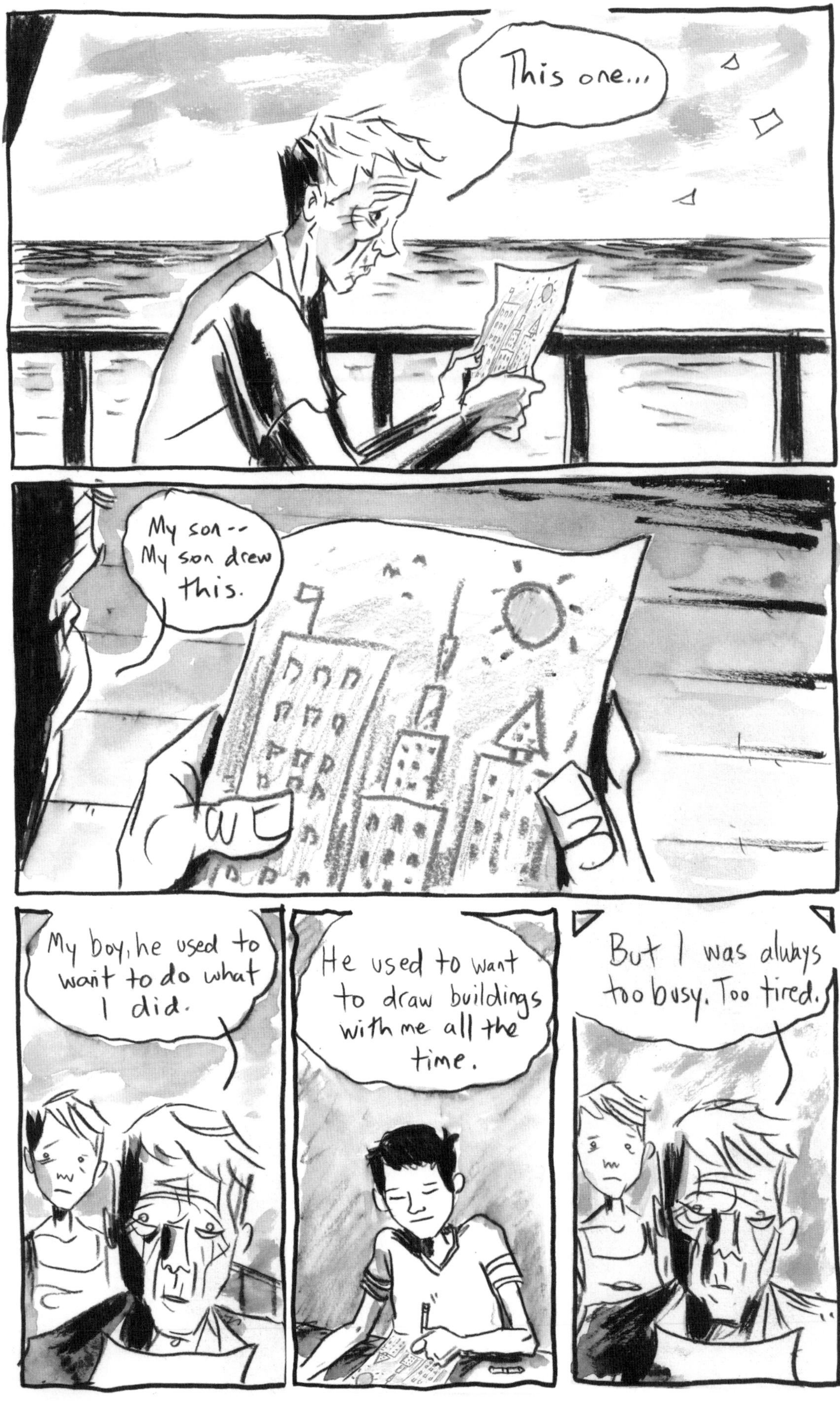
This one...
My son--
My son drew this.
My boy, he used to want to do what I did.
He used to want to draw buildings with me all the time.
But I was always too busy. Too tired.

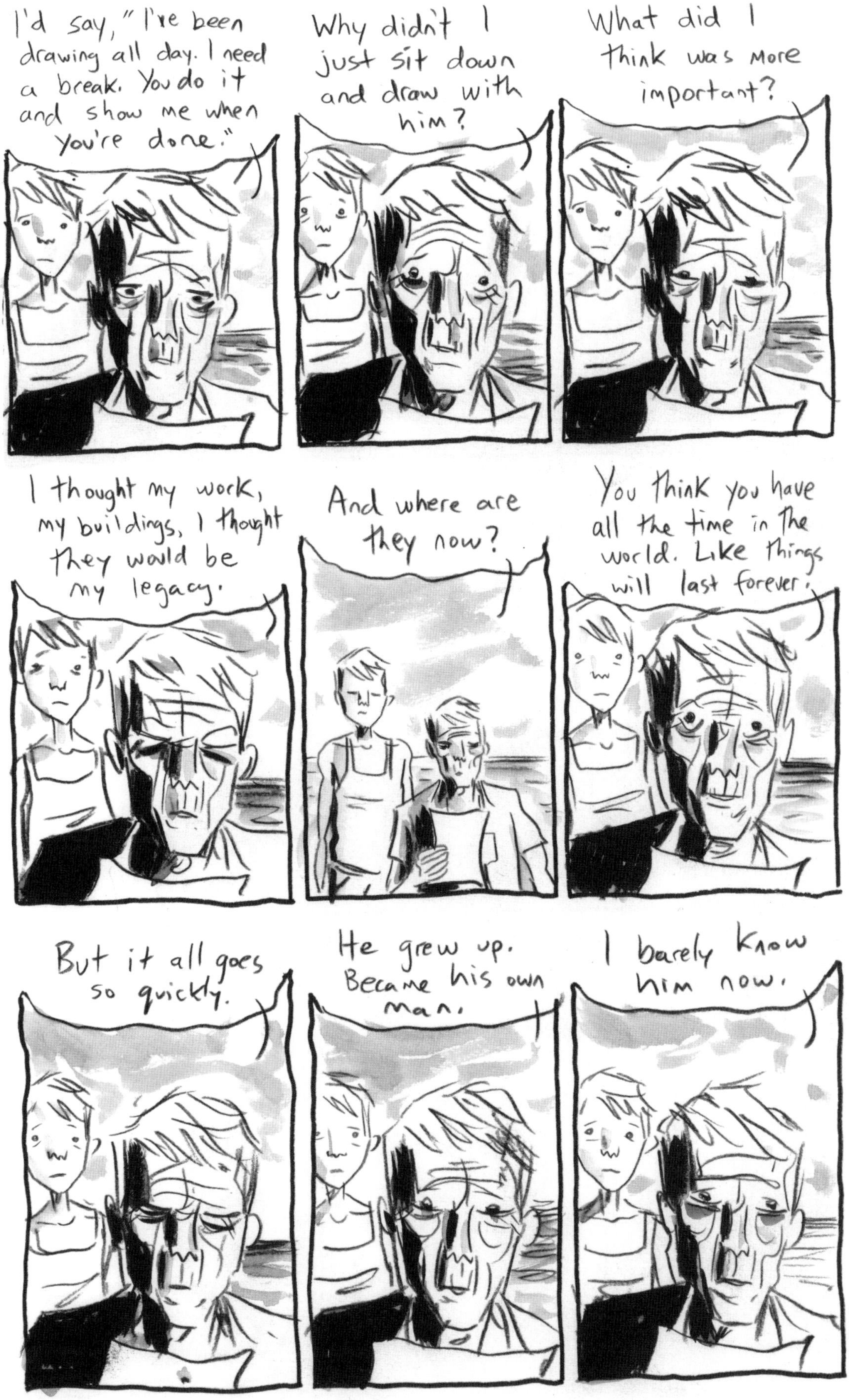
I'd say, "I've been drawing all day. I need a break. You do it and show me when you're done."
Why didn't I just sit down and draw with him?
What did I think was more important?
I thought my work, my buildings, I thought they would be my legacy.
And where are they now?
You think you have all the time in the world. Like things will last forever.
But it all goes so quickly.
He grew up. Became his own man.
I barely know him now.

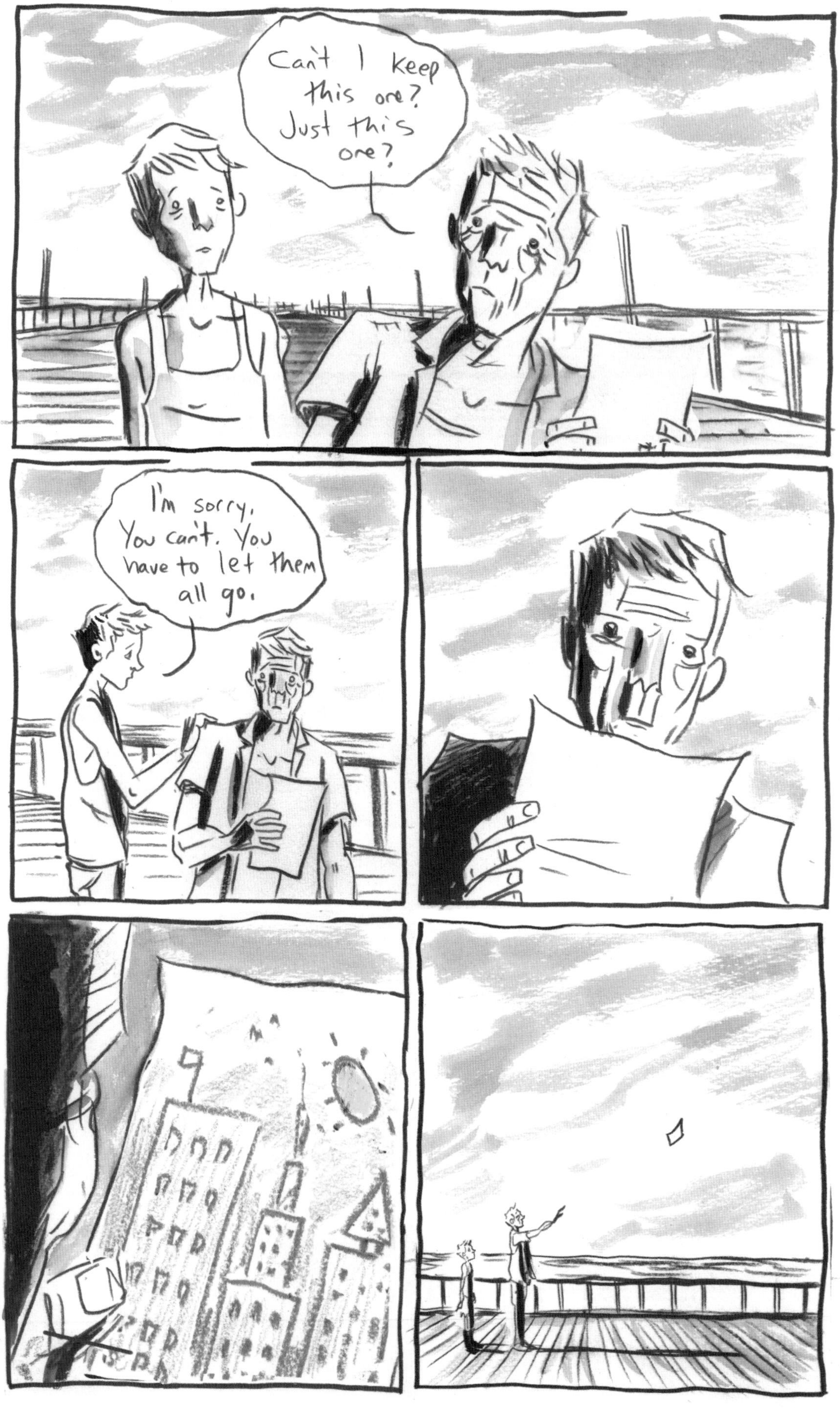
Can't I keep this one? Just this one?
I'm sorry, You can't. You have to let them all go.

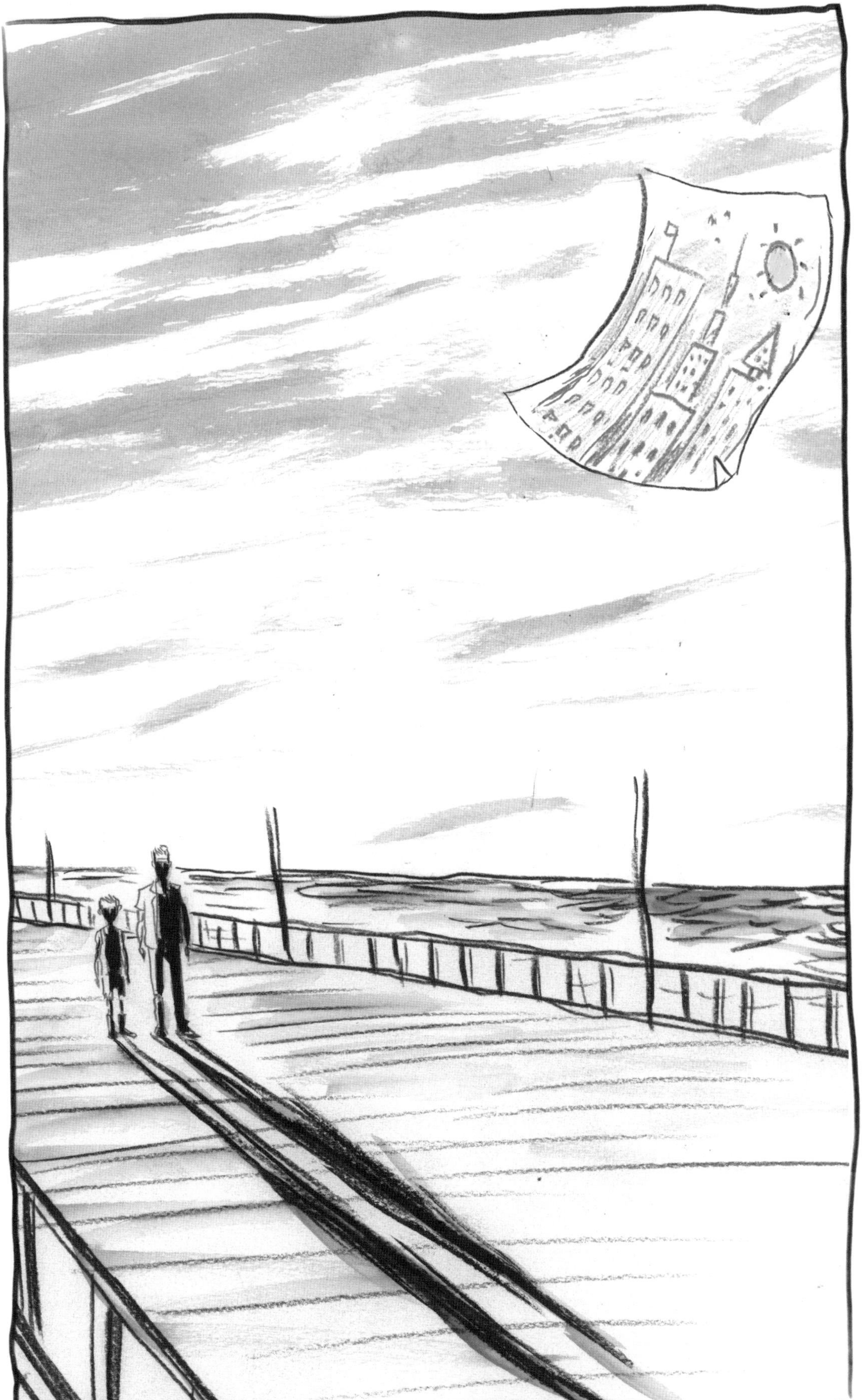

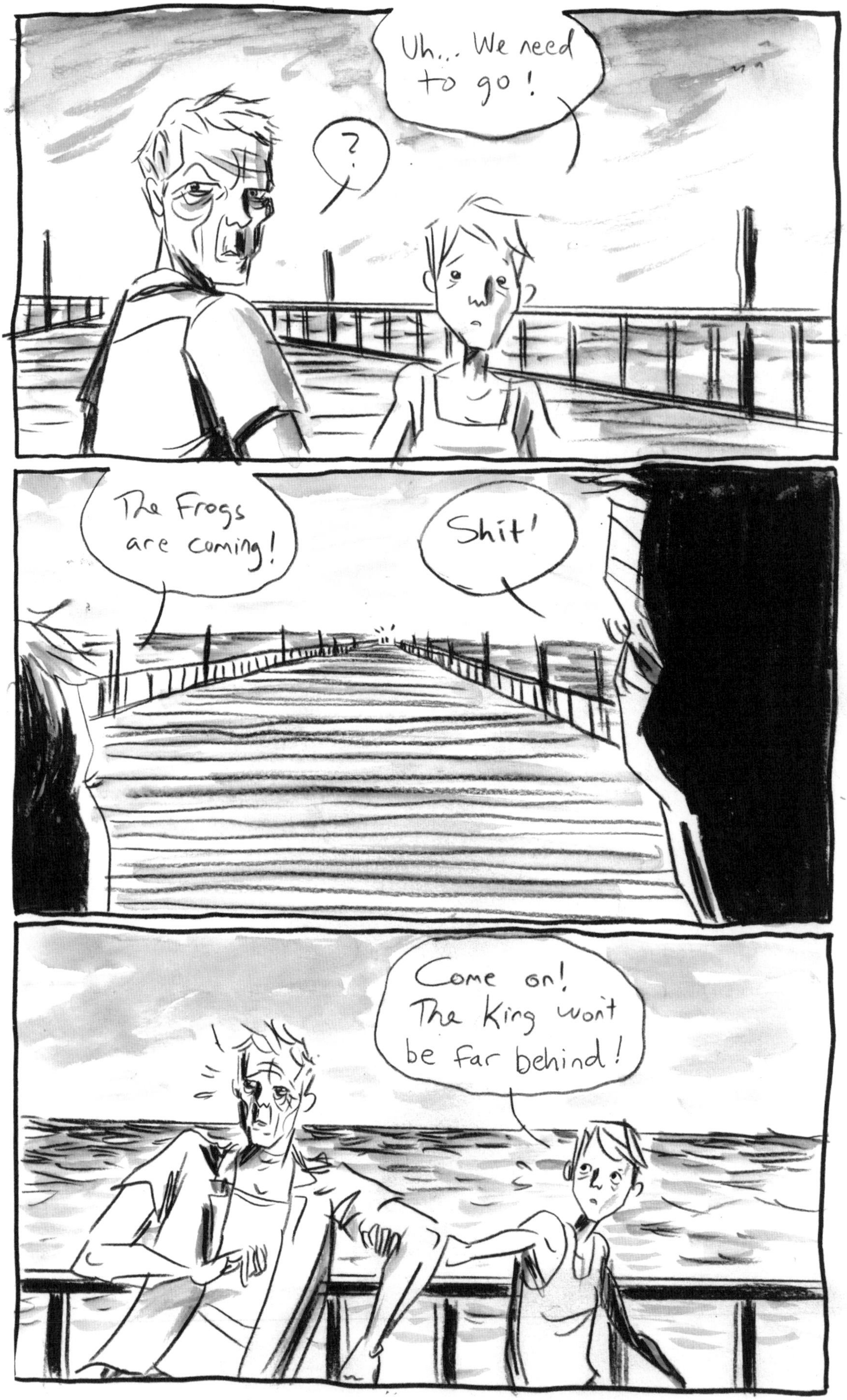
?
Uh... We need to go!
The Frogs are coming!
Shit!
Come on! The King won't be far behind!

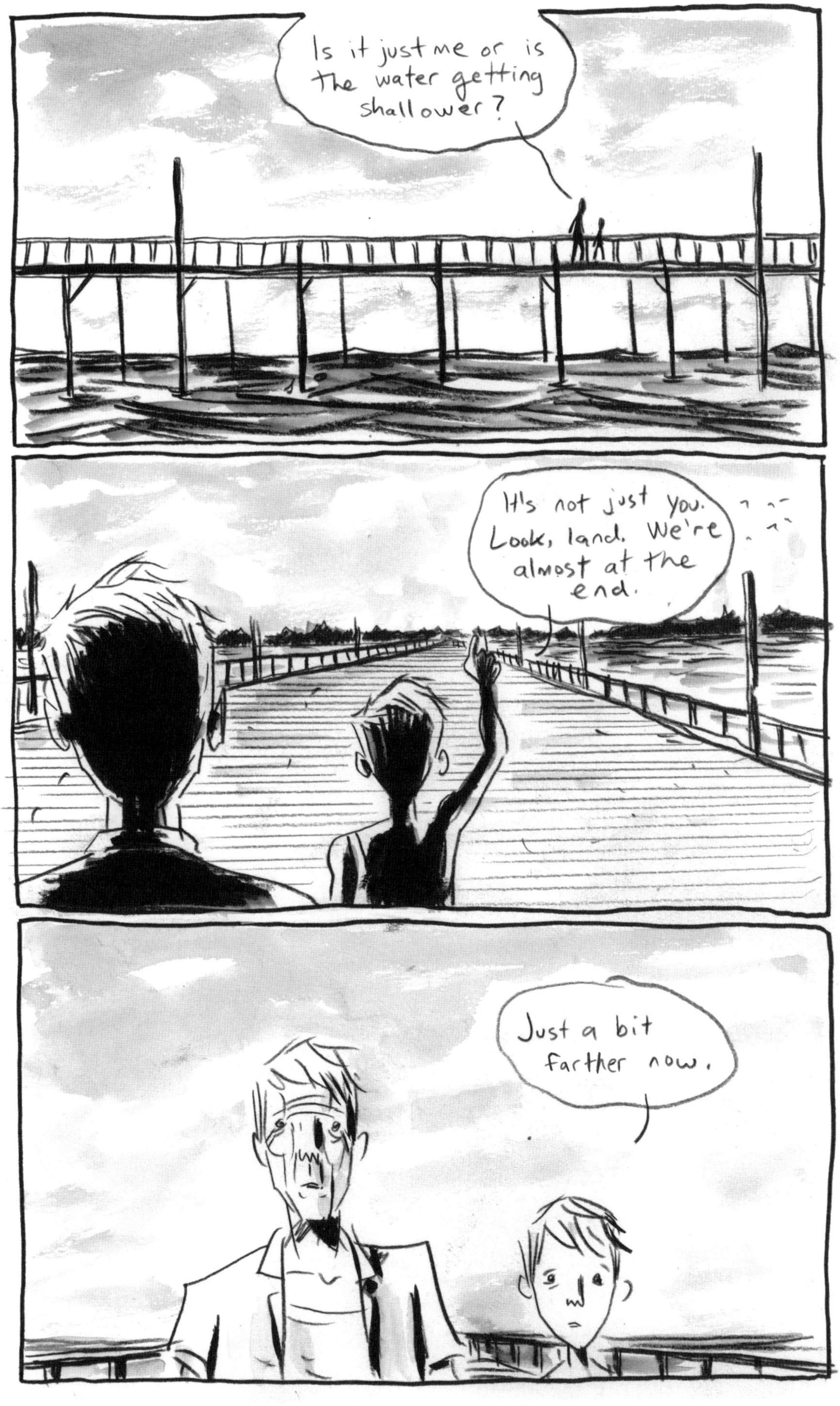
Is it just me or is the water getting shallower?
It's not just you. Look, land. We're almost at the end.
Just a bit farther now.

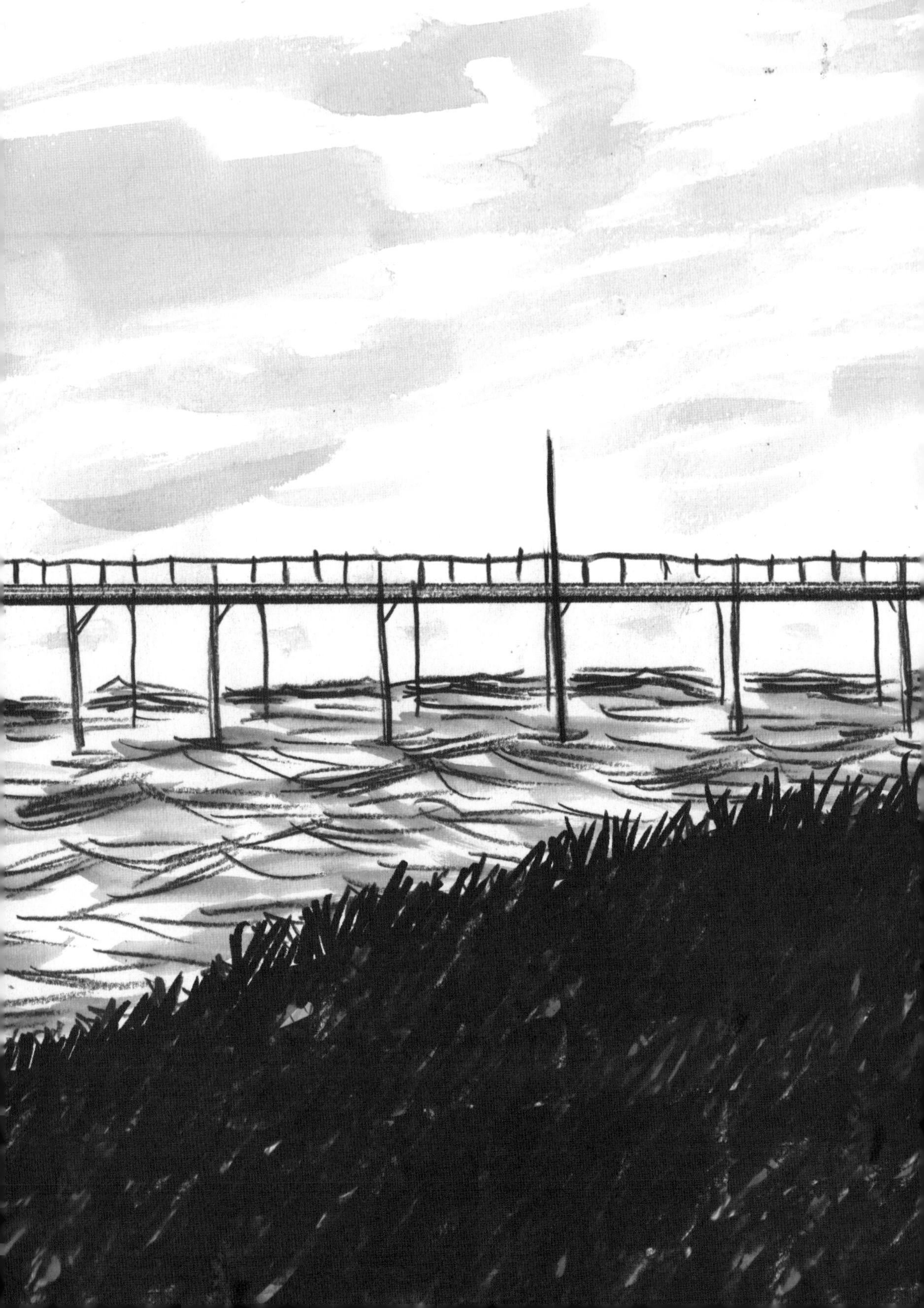

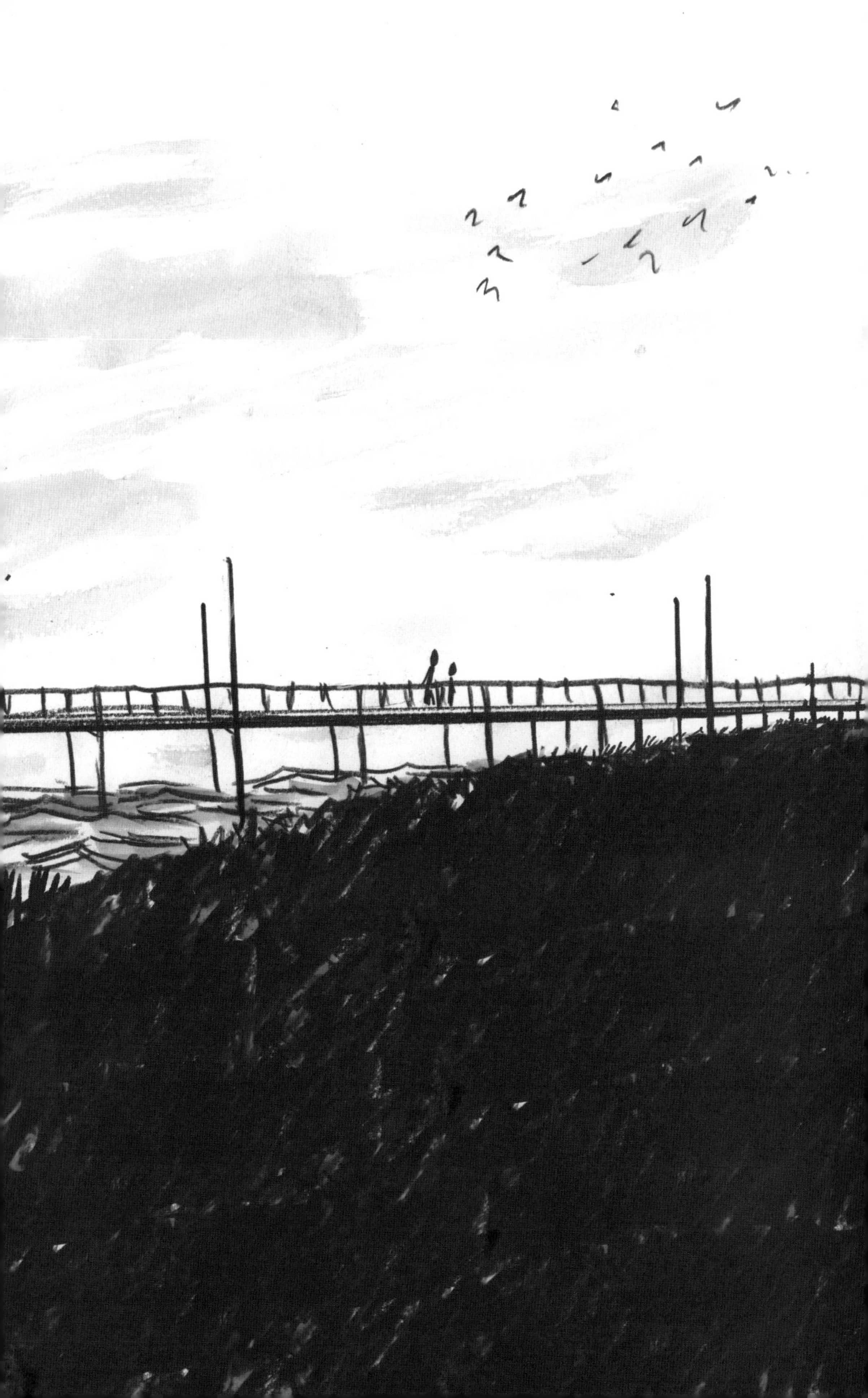

I think maybe we lost them, the frogs. I don't see them back there.

Hey, I think maybe I've been here before ... this creek?
We have...
Look.

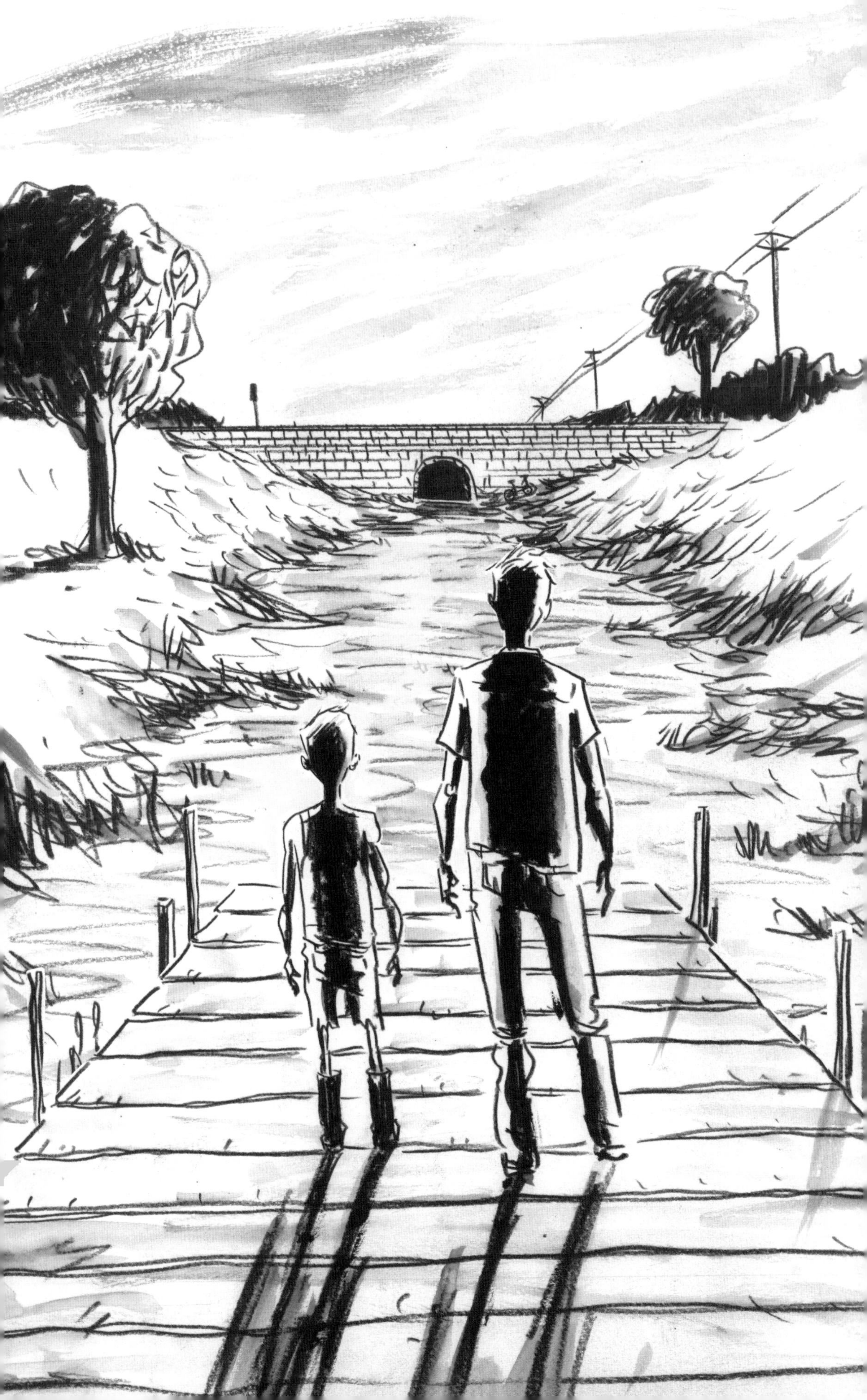

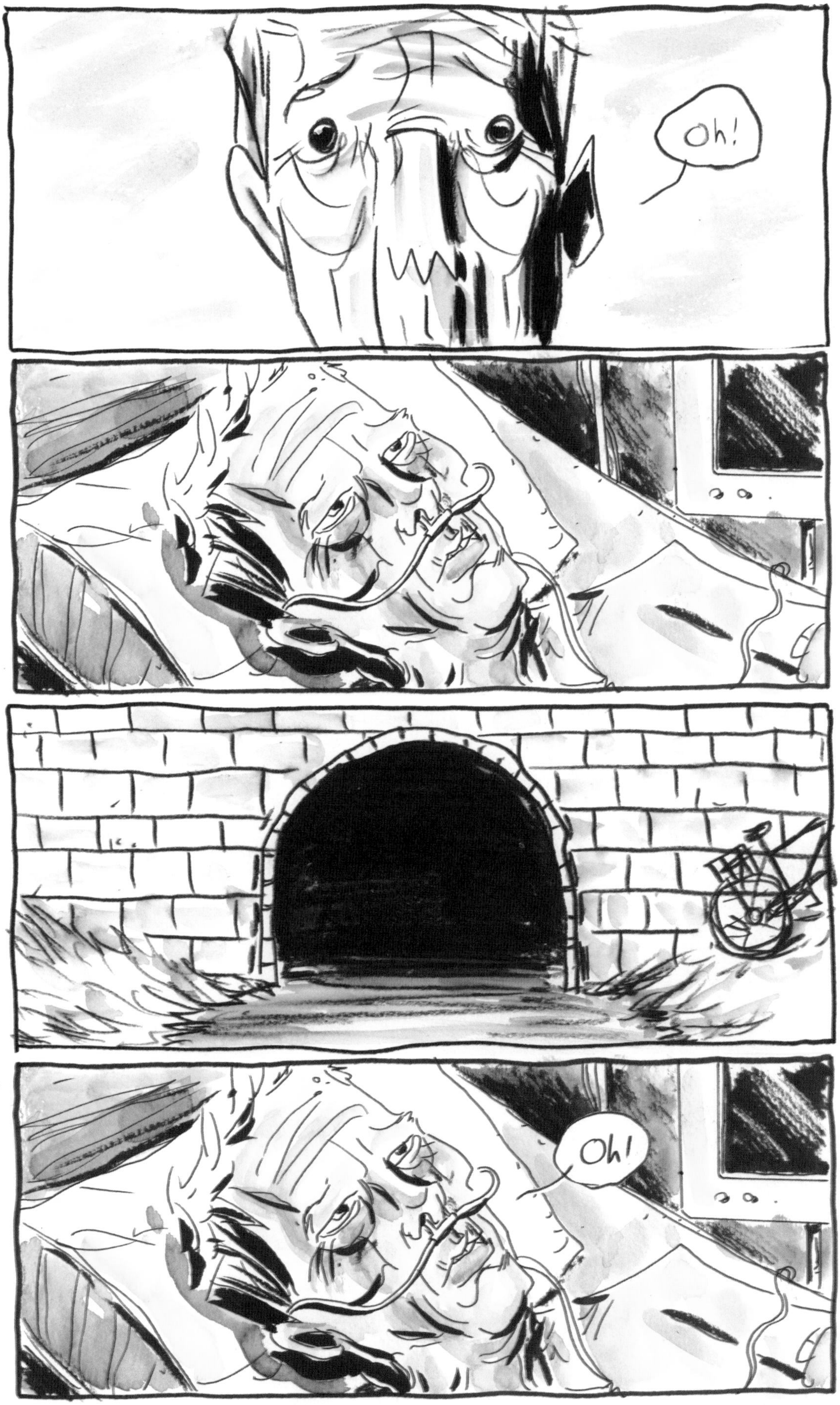
Oh!
Oh!

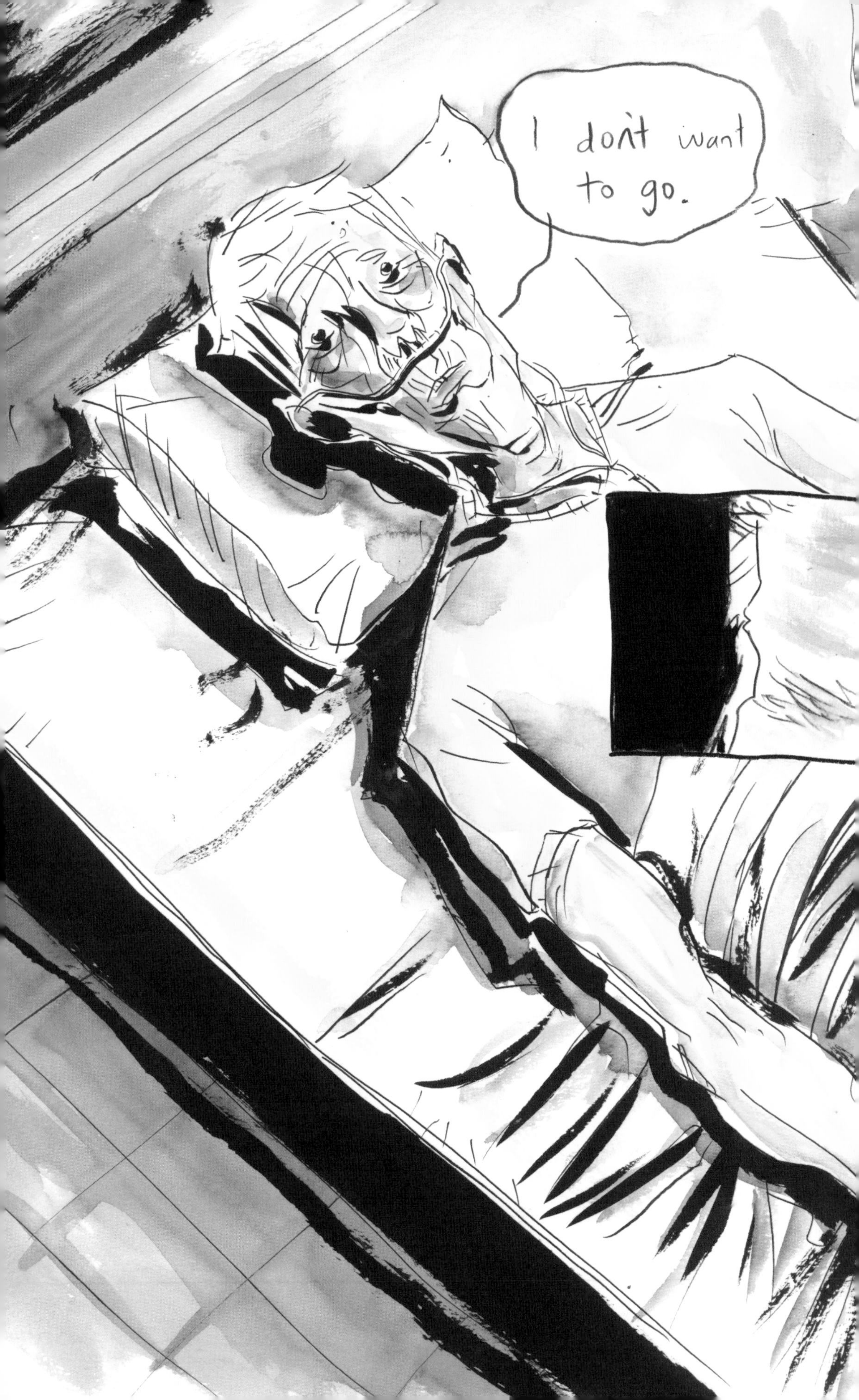
I don't want to go.

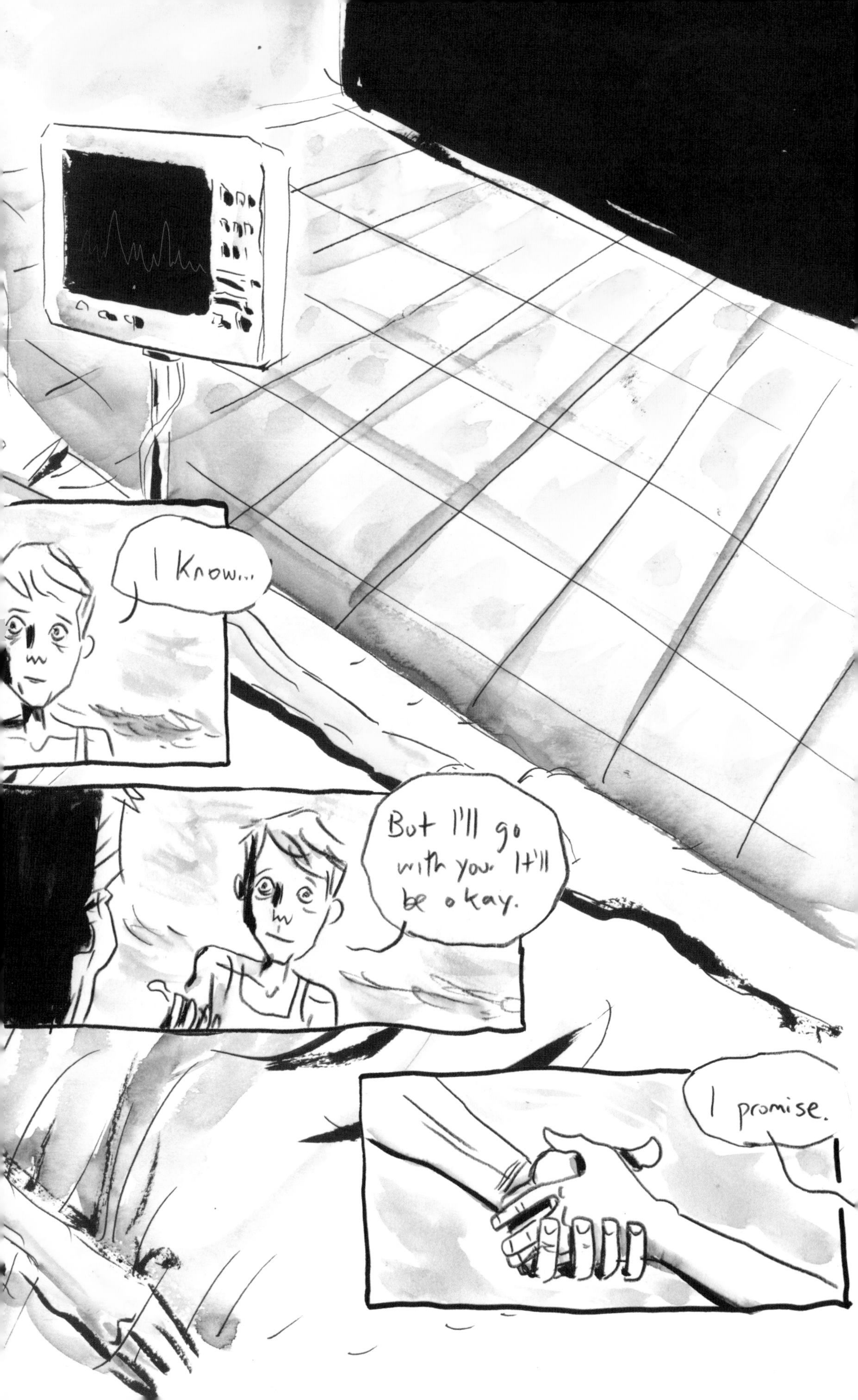
I Know...
But I'll go with you. It'll be okay.
I promise.

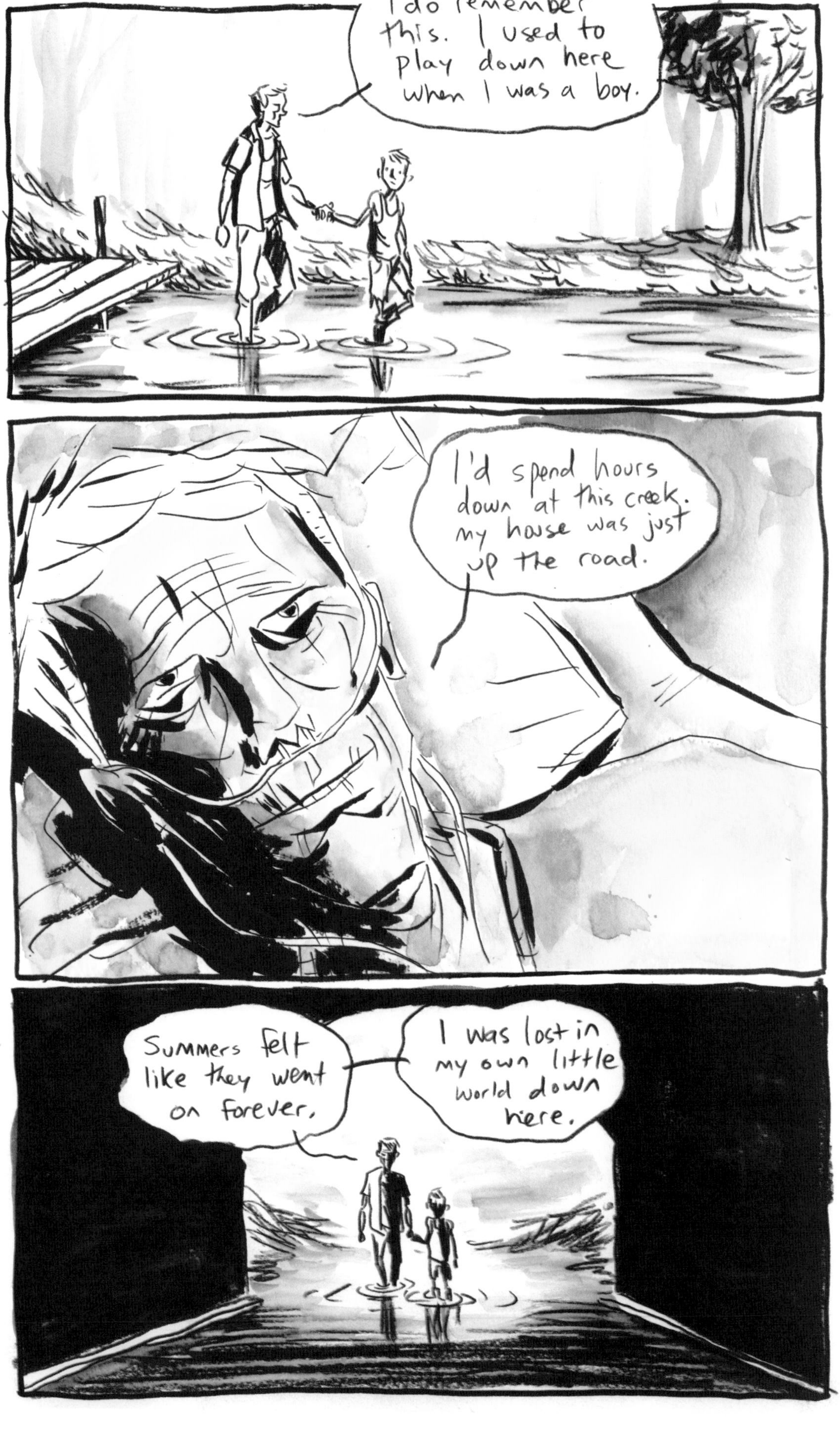
I do remember this. I used to play down here when I was a boy.
I'd spend hours down at this creek. my house was just up the road.
Summers felt like they went on forever.
I was lost in my own little world down here.

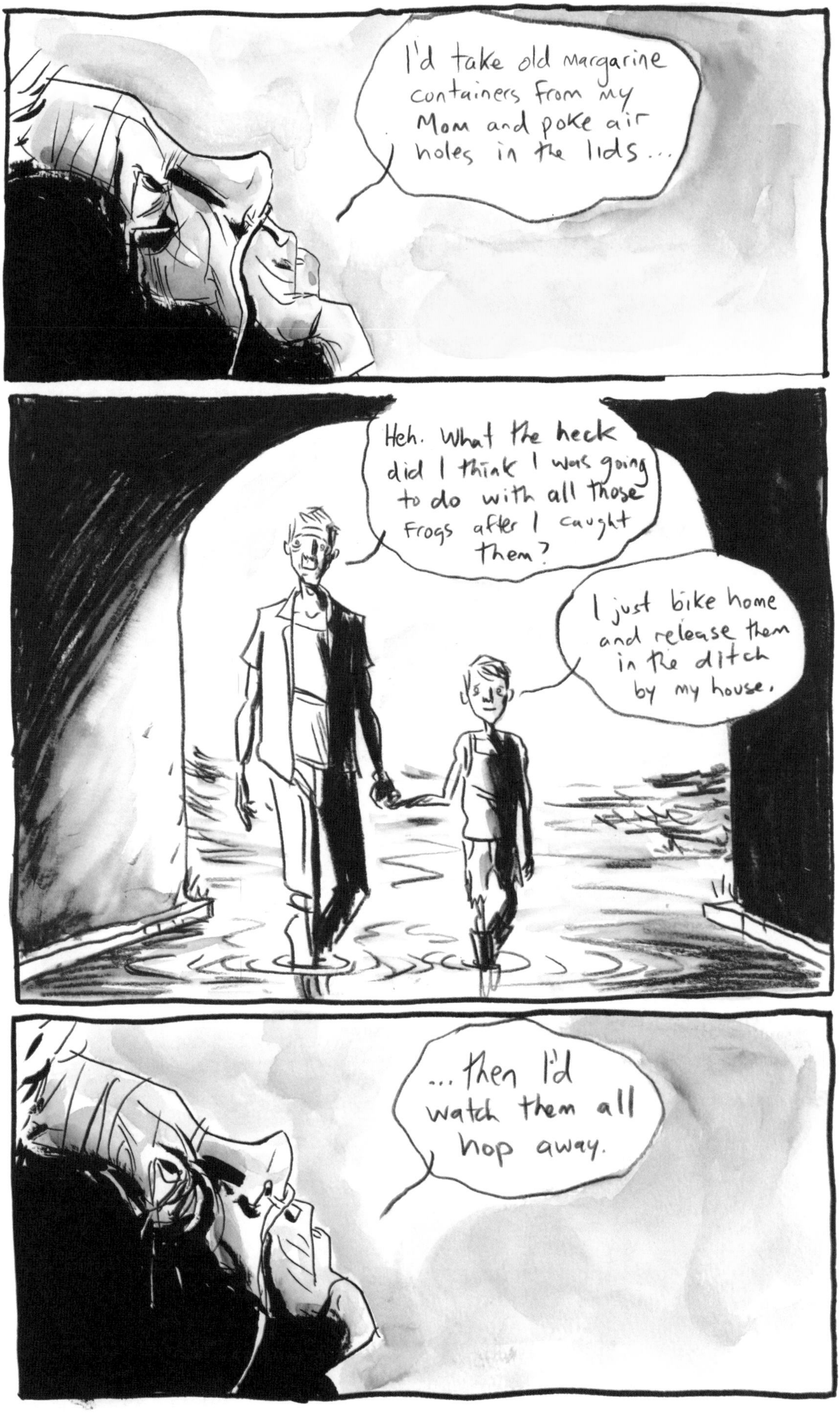
I'd take old margarine containers from my Mom and poke air holes in the lids...
Heh. What the heck did I think I was going to do with all those frogs after I caught them?
I just bike home and release them in the ditch by my house.
...then I'd watch them all hop away.

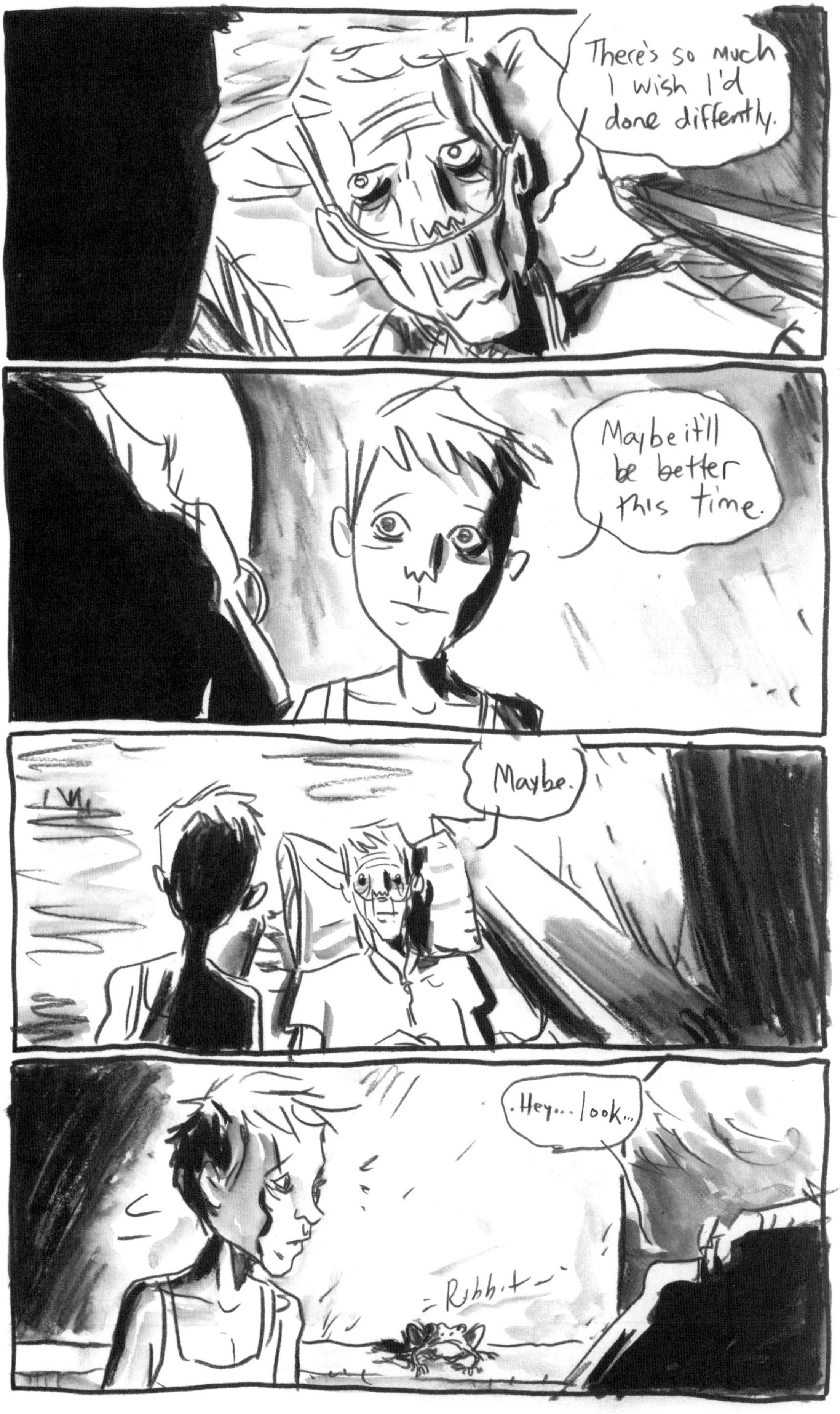
There's so much I wish I'd done diffently.
Maybe it'll be better this time.
Maybe.
.Hey... look...
Ribbit

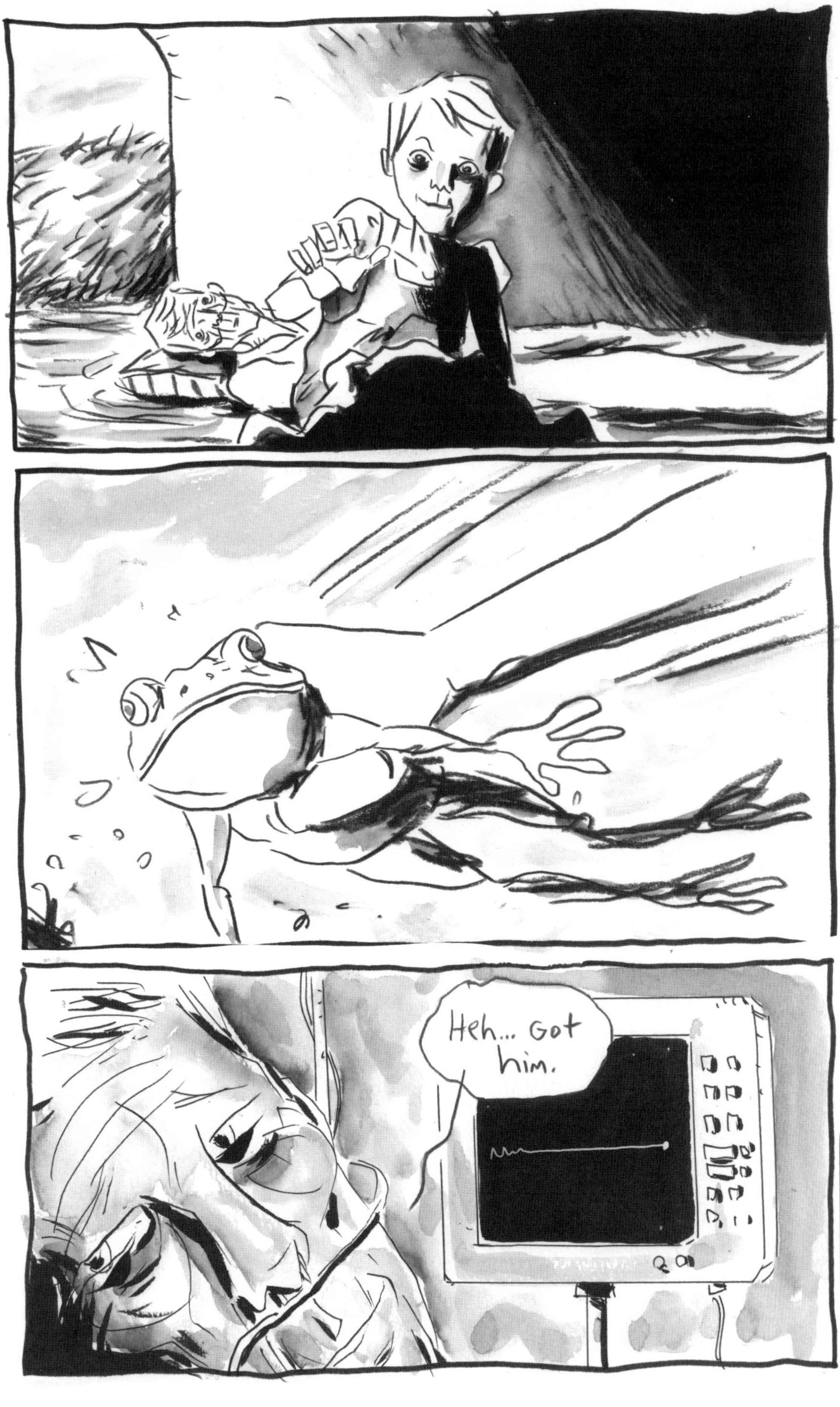
Heh... Got him.

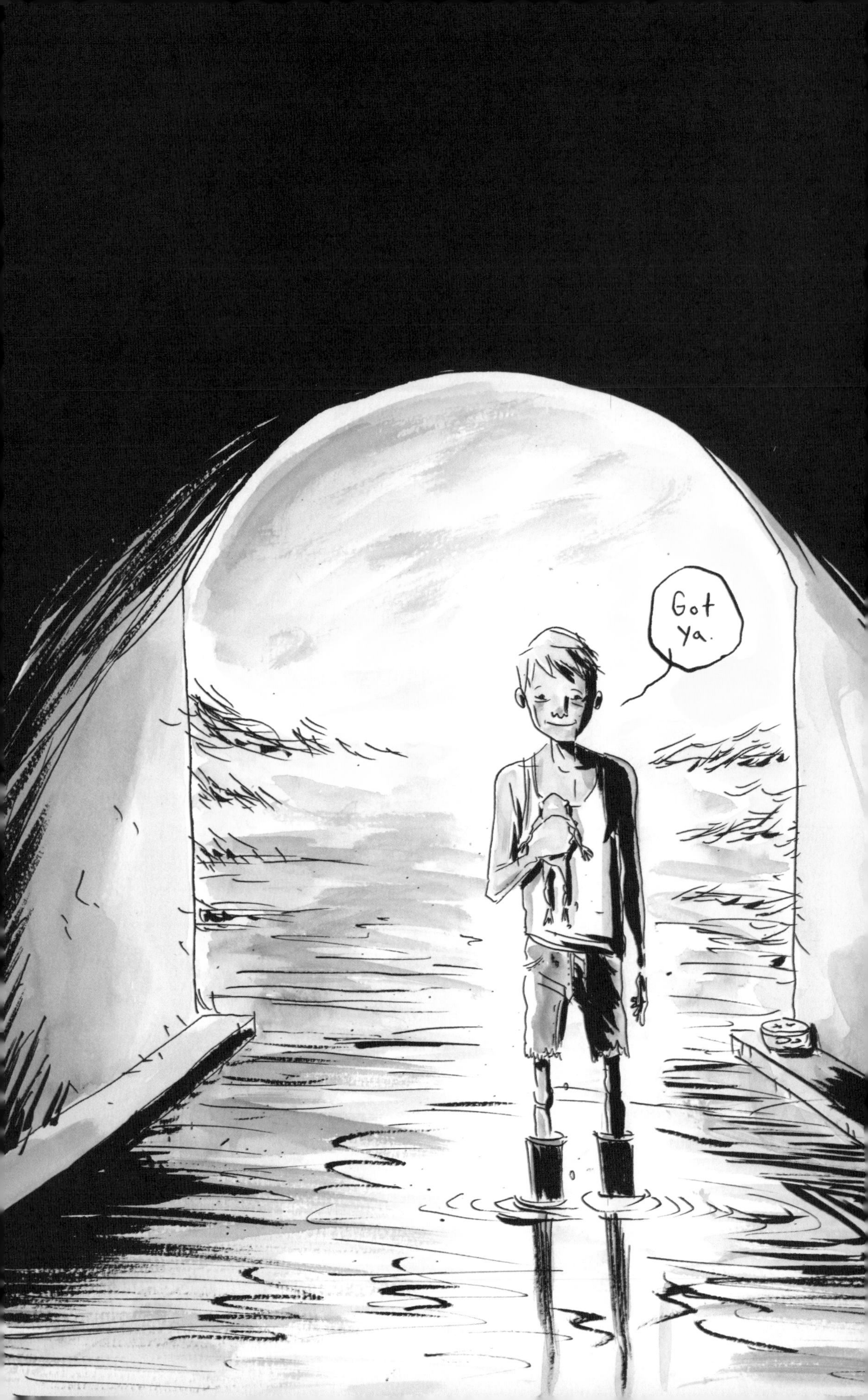
Got ya.

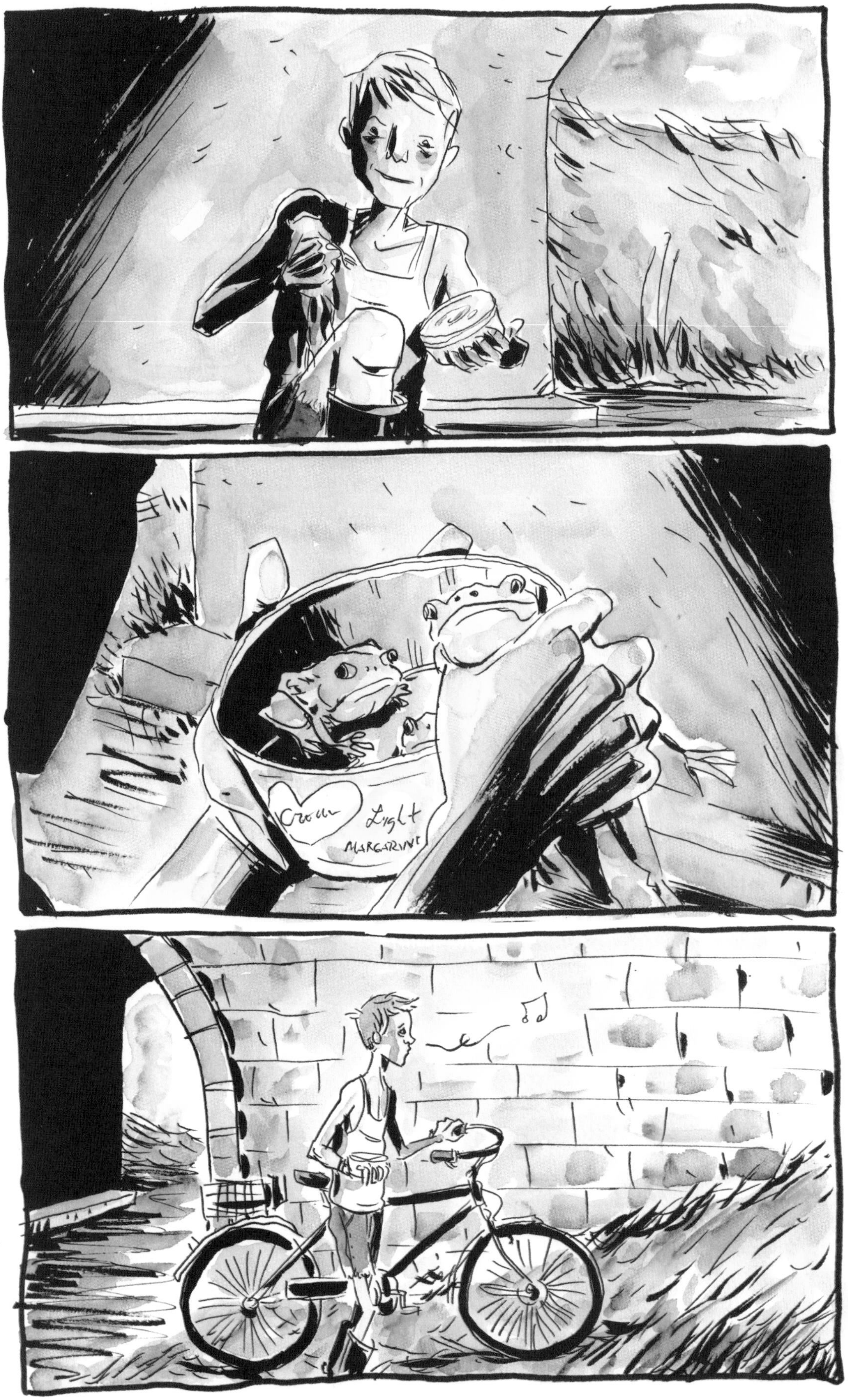
Crown
Light
MARGARINE

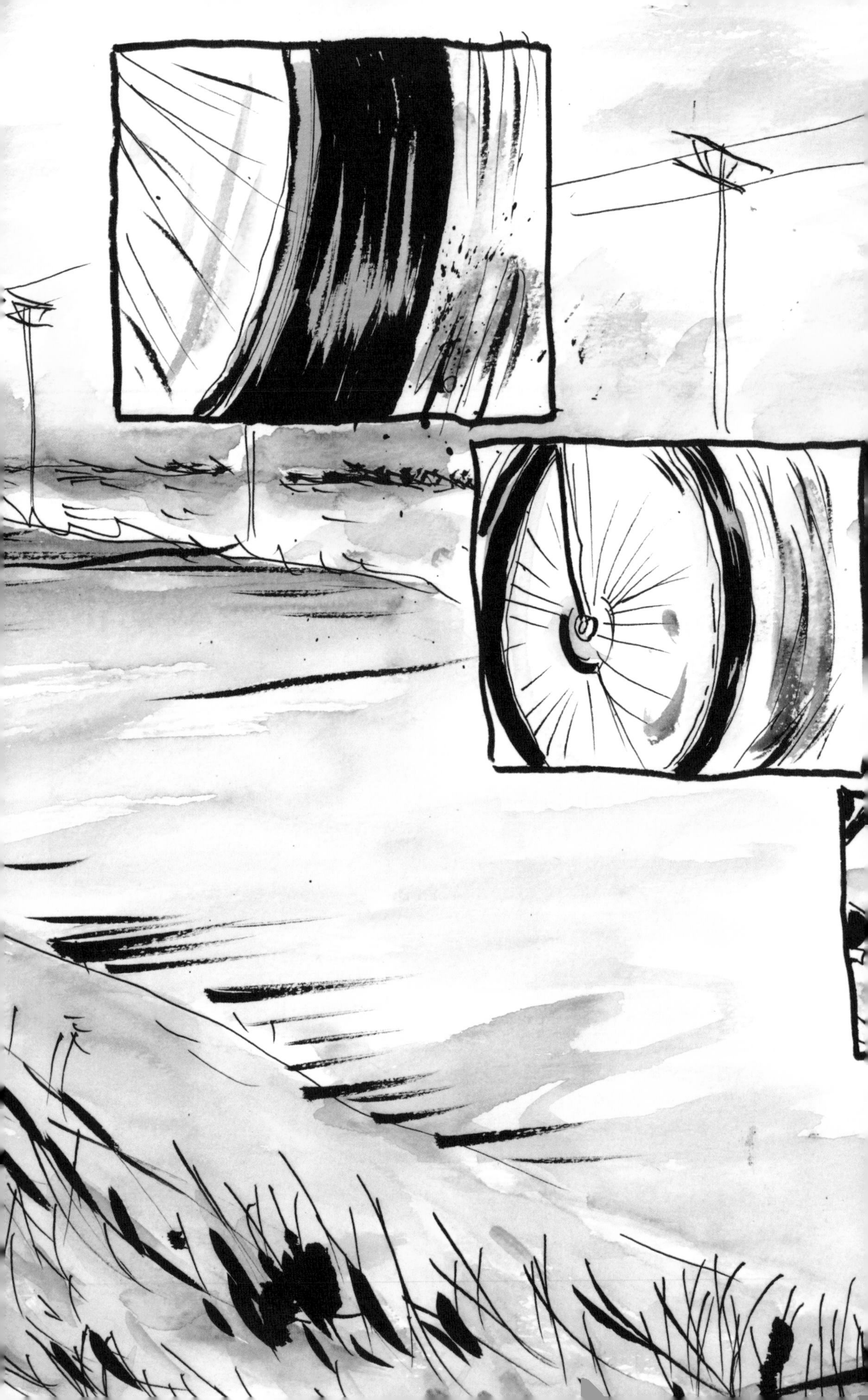

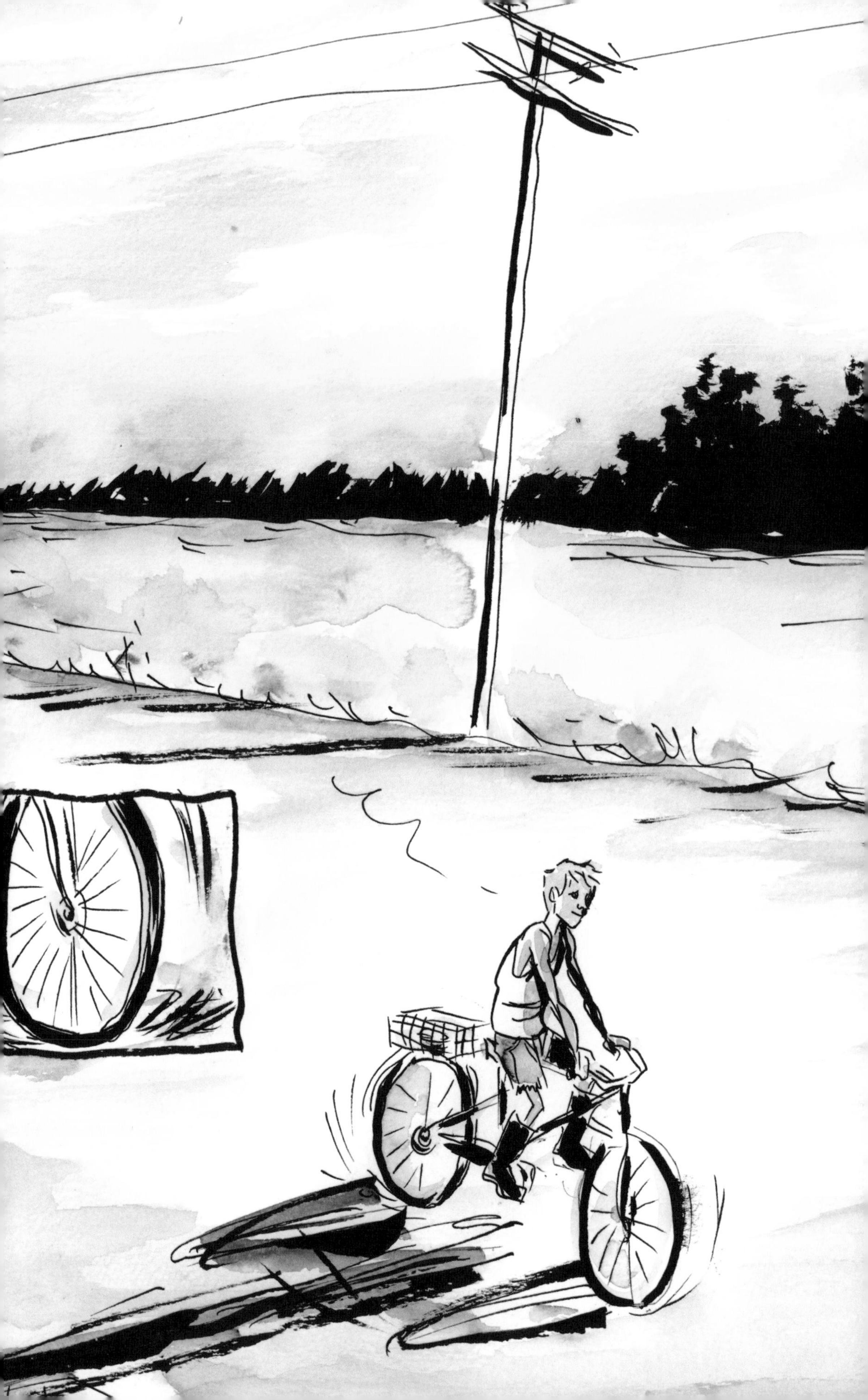

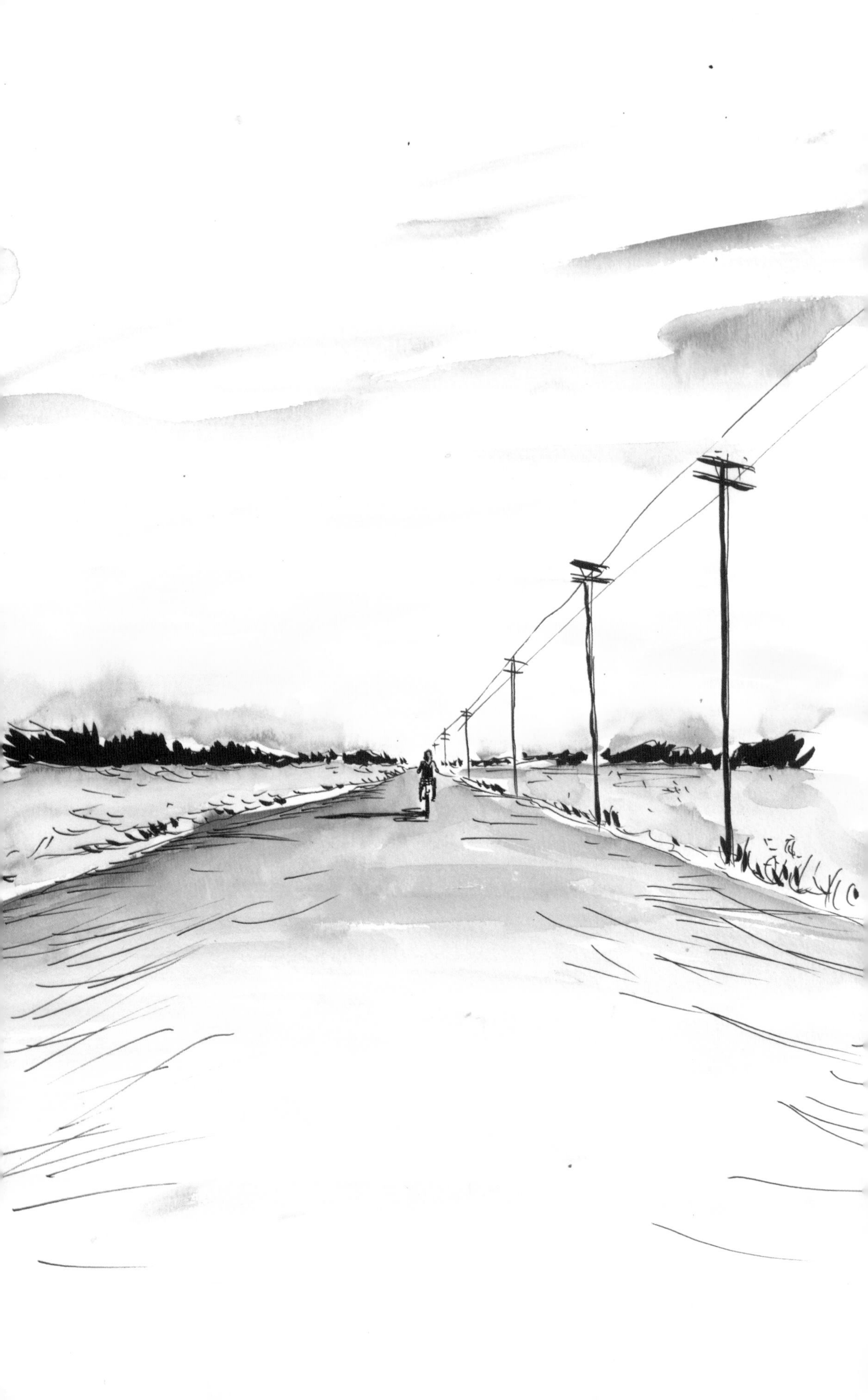

Special thanks to fellow cartoonists
Matt Kindt, Ray Fawkes, and Skottie Young —
for guidance, advice, and inspiration.

Jeff Lemire is the New York Times bestselling author of
such acclaimed graphic novels as Sweet Tooth, Essex County,
The Underwater Welder, and Roughneck. He has also written
extensively for both Marvel and DC Comics.

He also collaborated with celebrated musician Gord Downie
on the graphic novel and album Secret Path,
which was made into an animated film in 2016.
Jeff has won numerous awards, including
an Eisner Award and JUNO Award.

Many of his books are now in development for
film and television, including Essex County, Descender,
Gideon Falls, and Black Hammer.

Lemire was born and raised in Essex County, Ontario,
where he was a prodigious frog catcher.